A Magnificent Adventure

When He Who is Invisible is at the Helm

Cherie Young

WESTBOW
PRESS®
A DIVISION OF THOMAS NELSON
& ZONDERVAN

WestBow Press books may be ordered through booksellers or by contacting:

WestBow Press
A Division of Thomas Nelson & Zondervan
1663 Liberty Drive
Bloomington, IN 47403
www.westbowpress.com
1 (866) 928-1240

ISBN: 978-1-5127-4168-1 (sc)
ISBN: 978-1-5127-4169-8 (hc)
ISBN: 978-1-5127-4167-4 (e)

Library of Congress Control Number: 2016907617

Print information available on the last page.

WestBow Press rev. date: 05/25/2016

American Dictionary Of The English Language Noah Webster 1828

Word definitions have been taken from the Merriam-Webster Distionary/2015
Websters New World Dictionary/1966
The American College Dictionary/1966
(CreativeCommons Attribution-ShareAlike Licence)

Songs
Here I Am
Dan Schutte
Text & Music @1981, OCP, 5536 NE Hassalo, Portland OR. 97213 All Rights Reserved

Be Not Afraid
Robert J. Duffard, S.J.
Text & Music @ 1975,OCP, 5536 NE Hassalo, Portland, OR. 97213 All Rights Reserved

Amazing Grace/John Newton
Am I A Soilder of the Cross/Isaac Watts
Breath On Me, Breath of God/Edwin Hatch
He Lives/Alfred H. Ackley
Hold Me Fast Let Me Stand/ Mosie Lister
Little Wooden Head/Song from Disney's Pinocchio
The Comforter Has Come/William Kirkpatrick
The Eastern Gate/Isaiah G. Martin
There's Within My Heart a Melody/Luthur B. Bridges
This Little Light of Mine/Harry Dixon Loes
What a Friend We Have in Jesus/Joseph Scriven

Quotes
Louisa May Alcott
Jane Austin
John Bunyan
Walt Disney
Ralph Waldo Emerson
Benjamin Franklin
Foxes Book of Martyrs
Marie Neally
D.M. Moody
Nan Mooney
Beatrix Potter
Eleanor Roosevelt
Teddy Roosevelt
Uncle Ben/Spiderman
William Shakespeare
Charles H. Spurgeon
Mark Twain
Seargent Alvin C. York

Books
Nan Mooney's My Racing Heart
Edgar Prado and John Eisenberg's My Guy Barbaro

Thank you to Bill Metzger and the Bucyrus, Ohio Fire Department

Contents

Dedication

I dedicate these stories to you.

To you who are holding this book and reading these words, whether you are my family or my friends or a you I haven't met: I pray these chapters will bless you in a way that makes your travel and destination in life become even more magnificent.

I dedicate this book to you.

You are the one who awakened me in the night, inspired and guided me in the day, and encouraged me in my spirit to keep on keeping on and to never, never, never give up.

Thank you, most precious Holy Spirit of God.

Walk close to the Lord always and your life will be a Magnificent Adventure.
Stray to your own will and it will become a Diminishing Future.

—Marie Nealley

Preface

People grow through experience if they
meet life honestly and courageously. This
is how character is built. The purpose of
life is to live it, to taste, experience to the
utmost, to reach out eagerly and without
fear for a newer richer experience.
— Eleanor Roosevelt

Eleanor Roosevelt loved learning and her days in college. I have learned on the journey called Life that it too can be our college, a vast university of learning. Earth is a world of many testing grounds meant to prepare one for another world to come, for eternity. God is the frame of our universe, and we are the art of his creation. He, being the greatest of teachers, has given his students a gift of not only life, but also choice. We can grasp every lesson he lays before us, or we can choose to ignore his every thought. We can walk with him or away from him; it is in our power. Mrs. Roosevelt knew the importance of choice and what life has to offer. She knew the richness, honesty, and courage that choice would bring to her and others, travel that held nothing less than a magnificent adventure.

This story starts out as a way of wanting to be prepared to tell a story. In preparing, it too, became the story, and then the heart got involved. The mind can't be still. As the pages turn, it is the soul that ends up bearing all. It is a journey of childlike faith walked with a friend who will be there in the end. It is the friend and his influence that make this story ever so magnificent.

-1-

Marie

Marie Nealley always found a way to share a lot of her life, her dreams, and her faith with many people. She, being a writer, a poet, a painter, and a saint, told me on one occasion that out of all her works, she believed her quotation about where to walk was her greatest work.

It was our writings that drew us together; we each submitted open-forum articles to our local, small-town newspaper of Bucyrus, Ohio. It wasn't uncommon for people to write in and voice their opinions, or to have a story they wanted to be told. There were days when it made for good reading, and if it did not, just turn the page.

Marie and I first met through a letter she sent to me on a summer day in 1991. How excited I was when I pulled an envelope from the mailbox and saw the return address was *Marie Neally, 207 Lawn Avenue.* I knew she was a lady who often had articles of great depth published in our paper. "Why is she writing to me?" I thought.

Laying the other mail aside and pouring myself an iced tea, I went to the backyard and sat by our pond. I opened the envelope carefully so as not to tear any of the words inside. She graciously introduced herself and went on to say how she enjoyed an article I had written, and that she would love to get together.

Upon calling her, I learned she lived not far from my home. From hearing her voice, I knew she was a kind and gracious lady. We set up a time. Marie told me she would be waiting in her yard under a tree, and that she was. Two painted-metal porch chairs sat side-by-side in the shade, a place where we could talk for hours, and that's what we did. From that day forward, Marie and I were forever friends. I guess some would say we had kindred spirits. Although our lives were very busy, in thirteen years we never strayed far apart. She grew to know and care for my family and friends, as I did hers. Today I still visit on a summer day the same place the chairs sat, with her granddaughter Wendy.

There were a couple occasions I ate lunch with her and her husband Cleo. In 1994 Cleo passed away, and in later years Marie had to move from Lawn Avenue to the Altercare Nursing Home. She was then even closer to my home, and it was easier for me to pop in and stay a moment or two. Marie had become to me the grandmother I never had. The profound questions and wise answers she so freely gave away truly enriched my life. Her conversations were always on a practical and spiritual level.

On May 7, 2002, Marie was ninety-four and waiting for the facility's van to take her on an outing. As she bowed her head and fell asleep, she slipped away to a new home, heaven. I miss her so, but her words of faith, encouragement, and friendship live forever in my heart.

> *Care more for a grain of faith than a ton of excitement.*
>> —C. H. Spurgeon, British Baptist preacher

-2-

My Fortieth Class Reunion

As long as I could remember, there had always seemed to be sugarplums full of ideas dancing in my head. When I heard quotations and the ideas of others, maybe a unique story or a lesson of life, I had to scribble it down or jot a note, adding it to the plums' point of view. I often wondered if others had these knowledgeable plums dancing. Mine, quite lively at times, could become a little disorganized.

It wasn't until my fortieth class reunion, when all our children had left the nest, that I thought my sugarplums could have a purpose. As I mingled from table to table, there were many conversations going on, and I wanted to hear them all. I learned about everyone's grown children and their grandchildren. Many were getting close to retirement from their jobs as principals, bankers, surgeons, and teachers. I wasn't sure if the guys who talked about their International Harvester and Case tractors would ever retire. To me, the class of 1968 looked pretty good.

Pulling up a chair and sitting beside former cheerleader and dear friend Nancy Crum, I hear her talking about her writing career. She had come to an overwhelming roadblock and had decided to quit. I tried to encourage her, but I could see she had given up on her dream.

It was then I thought of Joyce Swartz Gibson, another classmate I had sat with on the bus for nine years. She was married to Bob Gibson, an editor of a large newspaper; maybe he could shed some light on this deadened dream of Nancy's? I hoped.

Bob came to our table, and when I introduced Nancy to him, the two began to talk. I learned Bob was no longer an editor but a professor at a nearby state college. He taught writing. It didn't take long to see Nancy was no longer interested; she had been over too many bumps in the writing world's road to try again.

Bob, remembering years past and my scribbles and jots, suggested I come to his writing class. I reminded him of my narrow-minded, nonfiction plums. He excitedly told me that was exactly what his next class was all about: nonfiction creative writing, plums included. "Think about it," he said, "and give the school a call."

-3-

Signing Up

Bob's words echoed in my mind: "Give them a call." Being the adventurous person I am, one afternoon I picked up the phone. After all, I could always hang up. My goodness, the Ohio State University did answer their phone, and they sounded like normal people. They transferred me to the English department and to a nice gentleman who was quite familiar with creative writing of nonfiction. "Did you already take the English course prerequisite?" he asked.

"I believe Mr. Gibson forgot to inform me of that," I told the gentleman.

"Well," he said, "don't give up yet. How well do you know the teacher? They are known to issue waivers for a class such as this. Give him a call and get back to me and we'll get you signed up."

I then dialed Bob. Before I could get all the words out of my mouth, he told me he would waive the prerequisite and encouraged me to get signed up as soon as possible. Being concerned about my English, I asked if I would be the dumbest one in the class. Bob chuckled and assured me that I wouldn't be. I wondered.

The next morning, I called the admissions gentleman again and informed him of all that Bob had said. "Great. You get over here as fast as you can, and I'll be looking for you. Don't forget your high school transcripts."

That got me thinking. It had been a long time since I looked at my high school grades. I was a child who lost her father at age seven. My mother then packed up my brother, our dog, and me, and we moved to a place where I knew no one. My many relatives with college backgrounds were now miles away, too far to be an influence. My mother and a new stepdad worked many long hours, leaving no time to pressure me to achieve. Therefore my sugarplums became dysfunctional and disorganized.

Now, pulling into the parking lot of my alma mater after forty-five years, she still looked good to me: Colonel Crawford High in the small burg of North Robison, Ohio. As I opened the glass doors, memories of the past renewed themselves. Entering the office, I could see our secretary had retired. There stood Margie Hoyle, a wonderful lady of our town. We shared smiles, and I told her my business was to pick up a copy of my high school transcripts.

"Are you going back to school?" she asked.

"If those grades will let me," I told her. I then explained that I applied myself much better now.

With another smile, she said, "Don't we all?"

I followed her into a file room. Margie pulled out a long drawer very near to the floor. I nervously said, "Don't look."

"Oh, you'll be fine," she assured me. She stapled the papers together and slid them into a manila folder. Sweetly, she handed them to me and said, "Good luck at school." In my heart she reminded me of my mother, who was no longer alive but had always been there to encourage me on when there came big bumps in the road of life.

As I walked back through the glass doors, a still, small voice from within whispered, "You should have tried harder, much harder, forty-some years ago."

"I know," I whispered back.

I got into my car and pulled out of the parking lot. I opened up the manila folder and pulled out the stapled papers and looked. I almost had to pull over and take a pill. I immediately wondered where I would hide these papers so my children or grandchildren would never see them after I died. Then I thought, "Forget the class for learning to be a writer. Forget the waiver. Forget Mr. Professor and the nice encouraging gentleman on the other end of the phone. It's all been in vain, and now it's a great disappointment." I could see where that door of opportunity was going.

My car kept driving down the road, and in no time I found myself pulling into the college parking lot. I parked exactly where admissions had instructed. Grabbing those stapled transcripts, I shoved them into my purse. I then made my way to another set of glass doors. When inside, I immediately could sense the order and smell of knowledge. I loved it.

I sat for only a moment before another door opened. There he was, the gentleman from across the phone line, all dressed in scarlet and gray. Yay, Ohio State! "There you are. Come right in here and let's see what we can do for you. Sit right down here," he said.

Some of what he was saying I heard, and some of his words were blocked by my fear of consequences and knowing how they do have a payday. As he was checking his papers, I was thinking of the ones stashed in my purse.

He went on to tell me how he hoped I'd qualify. He spoke of a wonderful lady who had left money for scholarships for people such as I. I wondered what type of people that might be—maybe old?

He gave me papers to fill out and sign. As I finished, he became excited that I was there and politely instructed me again where to park, the days and times I should come, where my class would be, and even where to pick up a college ID badge. I wanted to be as joyous as he, but knowing the information I concealed, I was once again afraid.

As he held out his hand to shake mine, he said, 'I guess that covers everything."

"Don't you need my high school transcripts?" I asked.

"No," he said, "I don't need to see those. You're fine. Don't forget now: you do qualify for the scholarship, and half of your tuition will be paid!"

As he bade me a pleasant farewell and all the luck in the world, I wasn't sure my legs could get me to the door. I was trying to act professional; little did he know I was in shock. Because of this nice gentleman, that door of opportunity was now wide open, and I knew exactly who was behind it all. The only words to explain what happened that day are *amazing grace*.

> *Visit many good books, but live in the Bible.*
>
> —C. H. Spurgeon

-4-

First Day of School

I had already told God I thought it would be best if we went to this state university incognito. Sure enough, we were told right up front not to be preachy in our writings, and I understood. I was there to learn how to write correctly, so maybe someday I would be able to write in another time and place of all the wonderful things God has done and been to me. I knew this was neither the time nor the place; I was here to straighten up my sugarplums that needed to dance straight in a row!

"I hear you're going back to school," said Dave Rowles, one of my husband's construction workers who was working in our home that day. Dave went on to tell me how he too had gone back to college and how great it had turned out for him. "You just go and have a good time. You'll learn a lot from the students, and they will learn a lot from you," was his counsel for a nervous, first-day, older student. You can't put a price tag on a kind voice of encouragement. It sure meant a million to me that day. Low self-esteem sat beside me in the car, and fear of the unknown filled the backseat. I'll never forget his words: "You'll learn a lot from the students, and they will learn a lot from you."

Dave's busy hammer continued to pound, and I closed the car door and pulled from our drive. I was heading down the road to my assigned parking spot at the Ohio State University branch in Mansfield. I cannot explain with words, but I knew with all my heart that I was going to a place that was appointed in this time for me. It was then I laughed within myself, knowing this was so out of character for me. It had to be someone else's doing. The doors of opportunity had opened so easily, I knew it had to be the power of my heavenly Father that was in control.

Pulling in to the campus and parking where I was told, I turned the car off and just sat for a moment. Gazing from my window, I saw many students walking here and there. They knew where they were going and what they were doing; I wasn't sure. I knew I wanted to learn how to write, and graciously I had been invited and accepted.

Getting out of my car, I walked to the building where I had been instructed to go and trusted someone would soon be telling me what to do.

> *When your will is God's will, you will have your will.*
>
> —C. H. Spurgeon

-5-

English 268:
Writing Creative Nonfiction

Winter 2009, Tuesdays and Thursdays
Professor Bob Gibson

Many years ago, I was taught that when fear sets in, "Fake it till you make it." Maybe I was a fish out of water, but I pretended to be secure and to know where to swim. Entering the beautiful outside corridor, I reached for one of the many handsome glass doors of higher learning. My fingers had almost touched the large metal handle when the door quickly opened on its own. There stood a tall young man with a smile that spoke of welcome.

Aw, he had just helped an old fish to swim upstream.

Thanking him, I hurried on my way. It was only a few steps before I saw a sign pointing my way to English 268, Creative Writing (thank you, God). Walking down another stunning hallway, I decided it was a good time to have a little talk with the sugarplums that were dancing up a storm. My tone was firm. "You plums have danced around all your life to many beats. Today I have gone to great lengths to get you all in a row and make you be who you are supposed to be. So today we will become serious, and this will be a day of change. You will learn there is a plum-line that needs to be followed. We, together, are going to learn. God bless you, sugarplums."

Entering the crowded room I wondered where to sit. Pulling out a chair beside a girl who seemed to be older than most students seemed to be the perfect place for me. It wasn't long before Bob came through the door and was ready to take attendance. It reminded me of grade school as everyone said "Here" or "Yeah" or "Yo!"

When my name was called and I said "Here," Bob explained that I was a friend of his wife Joyce, and now he had to be good! The class laughed as if it weren't possible.

-6-

School Days

As the days passed, we were told what was expected of us. It started to become a little overwhelming, maybe a lot overwhelming.

Action

Dialogue

Sensory Images

Do You Have Something to Say?

I Teach so You Can Get Published

Write to Be Published

Have a Thick Skin, but Thin Enough to Care

Be Personal

Write Every Day

You Don't Have to Fit into a Perfect Style

Write What You Love

Create a Scene that Walks a Motion

Don't Be a Know-It-All, Be a Question

Make Notes to Yourself or You'll Forget

Create an Attitude of Sound

Don't Worry about the Grammar and Just Write

Don't Care What Others Think, Just Write

Read a Lot; It Makes You a Better Writer

If You Don't Have a Good Idea, Write until You Do!

Give yourself unto reading. The man who never reads will never be read; he who never quotes will never be quoted. He, who will not use the thoughts of other men's brains, proves that he has no brains of his own. You need to read.
—C. H. Spurgeon

-7-

Essays

I set up my computer in such a way that my essays could venture out into the atmosphere of all the other brilliant, critiquing students in our class. As we wrote, the words went to all of them. We read each other's stories and came to class and told each other what we thought.

Oh dear.

My husband Alan and his worker Dave figured out how to hook everything up and get it running properly. As I look back, everything once again fell into place. It had to have been that same *amazing grace.*

Walking calmly and quietly behind our chairs, Bob explained the art of storytelling. The students zealously asked questions, and Bob profoundly had the answers. I could see the common ground this teacher had with his students. It was something I was unfamiliar with: decide on a topic and start writing, *now.* I thought I would be taught first and write later. The opposite occurred: we wrote first, then we were critiqued by the teacher, and then we were critiqued by fellow students. We learned through our mistakes. Oh, I knew I had much to learn.

As I looked around, everyone was typing stories. My hand popped up.

"Yes Cherie?" Bob said,

"What if you don't know what to write?" I asked.

Before I realized how silly that sounded, Bob answered, "Write about you, your childhood, and never forget the five senses: sight, hearing, taste, smell, and touch." Looking down at his watch, he then told us all to go home and finish our writings.

> *In prayer it is better to have a heart without words, than to have words without heart.*
> —John Bunyan

Who Is She?
My first writing

Who is she? That has little and has a need to give. That has a thought, but no change in her pocket. As the thought grows she watches her family discarding treasures of old. Picking up a cut glass pitcher of large size, she caresses to keep what they thought to pitch. Who is she? That has a need to give, collecting some paper and searching for the perfect box. As she wraps it so carefully and lowers it securely, taping, folding, and tying, who is she? Who is she? That now takes a small paper-like tag with a message penned that far surpasses Hallmark, ties it to a bow, and no trouble to drive to a destination even though the gas gage reads low. To arrive and cheerfully knock at the door with one hand, while clutching the precious treasure in the other. Who is she? When the door opens, it was not only the special treasure beaming with bows, but the eyes above it that spoke a thousand words. Who is she? I know you are my friend.

Friendship is one of the sweetest joys of life. Many might have failed beneath the bitterness of their trial had they not found a friend.

—C. H. Spurgeon

Stardom
My second writing

There I was in complete darkness, crunched in a ball, a knot in my stomach and all alone. But not really all alone, for on stage next to me was four other fellow clowns in their life-size Jack in the Boxes. We were waiting for the curtain to rise and the music we had been hearing over and over for months, and now was the last time for it to begin. It was our debut, our night to shine. For me the party begins when this night is over. I'm thinking I should have taken those dance lessons a little more seriously. I'm sure the other clowns know every roll, slide and shuffle-step-step. Maybe mom should have been a lot meaner.

Then as I thought the music should begin, I heard a loud whisper from the box next to me: "I have to go to the bathroom!" I was speechless and sure enough TaaaaaaaDummmmm, and it was time for all the Jacks to pop up onto the stage. I quickly glanced at the other four pointed-hat faces to see great joy of instant stardom, their arms and legs in motion as to a symphony. As for me it felt as if my heart was in my tap shoe and cement was in my legs. My head felt as though it could explode any minute.

'Hustle!' Words echoing in my mind, 'down, time to roll, head under, point those toes, don't get close to the edge of the stage.' I was remembering it all. I think I could have vomited, but instead I felt my hand in something wet. Oh, my fellow Jack couldn't wait, and if any disaster comes it won't be to her, Miss Stardom of the night. Finally, the song was almost ending, three skips, two slides and a jump back into the box. Remember, 'get those legs up, up, don't knock the box over, now, head down and grab your lid,' bang! There I sat alone with a stench about me, did I do it, did I pull it off, was I a star of the night? *Maybe I was.*

I'm number one.

-8-

Sixty Percent of Your Grade

As class went on, we continued to write small essays and learn flow technique. This was to help widen our story creativity. We were told there would be two main essays that counted for 60 percent of the semester grade. We were also graded on our class participation, verbal ideas, and critiquing. I guessed that I wouldn't be sitting back and just absorbing wisdom. (Shock one.)

We were then instructed that the main essays would consist of no fewer than five and up to twenty pages. That got my attention. (Shock two.)

I looked around to see the response from the other writers. There was none. They all seemed calm as cucumbers. Their papers were rustling and their minds were busy. I could see ideas popping off their brains onto paper. A bunch of brilliant younglings had half their essays already coordinated while I was still thinking, "What in the world do I have to write about that would fill five to twenty pages with intellectual charisma?"

I knew the room in which I was sitting was filled with talented writers and found myself falling short. I also knew this assignment was much bigger than "Who Is She?" and "Stardom."

The class had taken a turn—an uphill climb to an intellectual awakening. I was suffering from what my teenage son often reminded me was sin: the sin of *worry*! I knew college would be a challenge, but I had never dreamed that one such as I, walking in off the street, would be expected to write. Anxiety having a strong hold, I knew there was nothing else to do but the thing we so often do last: pray.

I said softly, "Dear God, my mind is blank. Please help me now, God. I need you to give me an essay of thoughts. I need you now."

A peace came over me. God did hear my voice. It was as though the sugarplums were immediately called to the front of the class and the teacher spoke an idea into their ears. It was as if I had found my niche in the midst of these younglings. An idea lay before my mind—an idea from God. He had given me an essay.

-9-

In a Year's Time
Essay 1

Did you ever have a song rob your heart? The words become a convincing message and the song is speaking just to you, as the tune becomes a mission and a direction. You begin to sense a power that is in some way unfolding an idea you yourself would have never thought of. As strange as this may sound, it is what happened to me on an October evening in the year of two thousand and five.

Alan and I were driving home from Frankenmuth, Michigan. We had spent time with our oldest daughter, Alana, and her husband Tom and also our first grandchild Jayden. Shopping at the huge Bronner's Christmas Store, we saw trains tooting and ornaments sparkling in all sizes, shapes and brilliant colors. Christmas trees were twinkling as we listened to the songs of the season. Being in a child's wonderland, Jayden could not even sit in his stroller because of the amount of packages stuffed and hanging on every available network of his buggy. Having our list checked off, there was now time to relax and just browse around. It was then I saw a gem of a purchase. "I must get this for myself," I thought and I did. It was a music CD by a young Irish lad I had seen on a public broadcasting station on TV. I loved his songs and his enthusiasm as thousands of people surrounded his stage to hear his angelic voice. His lyrics touched the hearts of young and old. I was so excited to now have in my hands the songs of this cheery, dancing, Danny O'Donnell. It was "Merry Christmas to me."

As we prepared to depart from the old German town, the gifts were all tightly packed into the backs of our cars. Hugging our children and grandbaby as we said our goodbyes, we then buckled in for a long drive home. Both cars driving their separate ways had hands waving and kisses flying through the air. Our last glimpse in the rear view mirror was the German-like streets with old black lantern lampposts glittering in the night. What a wonderful day it had been. Not to let myself get melancholy, I immediately popped in my new CD and sat back to relax as we journeyed home, listening to all the songs, some being peppy and others calming to the soul. Little did I know there were two songs that would kidnap my soul.

Here I Am, Lord

I, the Lord of sea and sky, I have heard my
  people cry.
All who dwell in dark and sin; My hand
  will save.
I, who made the stars of night, I will make
  their darkness bright.
Who will bear my light to them? Whom
  shall I send?
Here I am, Lord. Is it I, Lord?
I have heard you calling in the night.
I will go, Lord, if you lead me. I will hold
  your people in my heart.

As I listened to this captivating song, I knew the lyrics alluded to the story of Samuel in the Bible. But this night while driving home from Michigan, it was as if a scroll was lowered down from the heavens, and on the parchment of enchantment, a mission was unfolding within my thoughts. As Alan was joyfully talking on his cell phone, checking on the kids' departure, all I could hear was the words of this song. Tears began to moisten my cheeks. I could see nothing from my window but a black sky. Over and over, this message in song became clearer to my understanding: go find him.

I, the Lord of snow and rain, I have borne
  my people's pain.
I have wept for love of them. They turn
  away.

I will break their hearts of stone, Give them
hearts for love alone.
I will speak my word to them, Whom shall
I send?
Here I am, Lord. Is it I, Lord? I have heard
you calling in the night.
I will go, Lord, if you lead me. I will hold
your people in my heart.

—Dan Schutte

I cannot explain it, but I knew the song was talking about my brother's son, Steven. I knew for some reason I was to go to him. I could sense a concerned love that was much greater than even the love of a mother. Was God speaking through a song?

I began to think of Steven and his losses in life, the hurt he bore. Many bad choices had brought him into darkness, a darkness that could cause him much harm. Then I began to fear what this mission may entail. Once again fear of the unknown made itself present. Fear because of my weaknesses and fear of what may lie ahead. Even so, I think I would have gone crazy if someone had told me I couldn't go. A messenger in song had been sent concerning Steven, and a mission lay ahead. How did I know this? There are times you can't explain with earthly words, but through faith you know, and then you must believe and trust.

Faith is the evidence of things not seen and the substance of things hoped for.

Through faith one can understand our world is framed by the word of God. By faith Abel offered to God a more excellent sacrifice. Noah was warned and moved with fear as he prepared an ark. Through faith Sara received strength to conceive and by faith Abraham when he was tried offered up Isaac, Moses by faith, refused to be called the son of Pharaoh's daughter, choosing rather to suffer affliction with the people of God. By faith the walls of Jericho fell down and by faith, the harlot Rahab perished not with them that believed not, when she received the spies with peace.

(Heb. 11: 4, 7, 11, 17, 24, 30, 31)

Did God have a plan? How could I imagine such a thing? Then there was a second song.

Be Not Afraid

You shall cross the barren desert, but you shall not die of thirst.
You shall wander far in safety though you do not know the way.
You shall speak your words in foreign lands and all will understand.
You shall see the face of God and live.
If you pass through raging waters in the sea, you shall not drown.

*If you walk amid the burning flames, you
shall not be harmed.
If you stand before the power of hell and
death is at your side,
Know that I am with you through it all.
Blessed are your poor, for the kingdom
shall be theirs.
Blest are you that weep and mourn, for
one day you shall laugh.
And if wicked tongues insult and hate
you all because of me, blessed, blessed
are you!
Be not afraid. I go before you always. Come
follow me,
And I will give you rest.*
—Robert J. Dufford, S.J.

Although the mission was foggy, the command was clear: Go

(1 Sam. 3:4; Matt. 5:1–12; Matt. 28:20).

That same evening while Alan was sleeping, I slipped quietly out, started the car and found myself on the square of our small town. Laughter and music echoed as the uptown doors swung open. Smoke and liquor were the perfumes of the night. "Excuse me, is Steven Cramer in there?" I asked.

"No, he's next door," yelled a man.

Walking into an alley to the back door of another bar called the Crazy Fox I knocked again, "Is Steven Cramer there?"

I waited a moment and there he came, a tall six foot three, clean-cut, good-looking guy in his stonewashed jeans and white Nikes. I could see his surprise and I could feel mine. Also there was a presence of compassion on both parts, a thirty-seven-year-old nephew to his fifty-five-year-old aunt. As he stepped outside, my conversation to him was, "I just had to come." He told me he was fine and wasn't sure what I meant. I wasn't sure what I meant, although I could see his lifestyle was taking its toll and I wondered if the song knew more than he and I.

Steven seemed to accept my concern graciously and we decided the help he needed would be a cleaning lady every Monday. Strangely enough I was excited, and he too seemed as if that was great. Who would have thought that visiting a bar in the middle of the night and getting a weekly cleaning job would meet the need of a heavenly mission? Giving Steven a big hug on the sidewalk of our square and telling him I'd see him Monday, we parted ways for just one day.

Driving home I couldn't help but remember I was Steven's first babysitter. I changed his diapers and put all sorts of hats on his head before he could even roll over. He watched his uncle reload shotgun shells, so young he didn't even know what the clicking contraption was. We always spent birthdays and holidays together, and how he loved the candlelight Christmas Eve service at church. Steven's parents divorced when he was eight, and I remember his teen years were a bit rough. His grandmother, my mother, always seemed to know where he was and what he was doing. It was one of those nights she called me to rescue him from what she knew to be a wild party. I'll never forget his face when they yelled across the room, "Steven, your aunt's here." Surprisingly he went straight home!

It was a shock to hear Steven was not going to graduate high school because of failing government class. Everyone knew he was just not applying himself. After calling his teacher and studying once a week for tests, Steven passed with flying colors. I was so excited and proud of him, I drove to his school before government class and tied the biggest green-frog helium balloon on the back of his chair. It ribbited and had the words "Congratulations! You did it!" written on it.

It was a joy when he'd pull in our drive with a new vehicle. I could always see myself in the shine of the fenders. We'd all get a ride and a hug, and then off he'd go.

I remember my stepdad and I cleaning out a burned house of a friend, and everything had to get out in one day. After exhausting every avenue to find a truck, I thought of my nephew. It was only minutes and there he was with a friend, a smile, and those eyes of compassion to fill my need. Now pulling into the garage and feeling very tired, I knew I would forever treasure my memories of my nephew and our relationship. As my head touched my pillow and my eyes closed, I wondered what Monday would bring.

Monday morning, my first day at 260 Wayne Avenue, I met Todd the roommate and learned he earned his room by paying the utilities. Monday being garbage pickup, I had to work quickly. There were a few times I ran late in getting to work and would find myself running down the middle of Wayne Avenue, yelling, "Wait!" The loud sound of brakes would squeak in a halting stop, as the three garbage men hanging from the huge truck waited for my additional, overstuffed, black bags. I was adding to the five they had already picked up. It took several weeks and many bags just to start our wonderful makeover of the prominent bachelor pad.

Todd thought the trashcan was the floor under the kitchen table. He worked in a factory, and the dirt he brought home made his white computer keys a gray-black tone. After a couple weeks, the computer went on the blink, and I saw Todd had bought a new keyboard. I often wondered if using Windex on all those keys would hurt, but didn't say anything. There were days the boys would tell me they couldn't find things, thinking I had discarded or misplaced them. I was so careful not to do such a thing. I would ask, "When was the last time you saw the lost article?"

They would answer, "Three years ago."

It was funny how Todd would blame Steven and Steven would later blame Todd for all the untidiness—and when I say untidy, I'm being very kind.

Razz the dog was never excited about Mondays. He knew it was time for his shaggy, shedding body to go out for the entire day, to bask in the sun or the shade—it was his choice.

There was a day Steven forgot to leave the front door open. Unable to get in, I decided to focus on straightening the garage.

This was a job all in itself. What a challenge! I was looking forward to the miracle I was about to perform. Again, bag after bag, tie them up and set them out on time for my garbage-collecting friends. Little did I realize my nephew would be getting a call of rage in the middle of his evening out. Steven calmly informed me about his unhappy roommate. I felt awful and sure didn't want to make trouble between Steven and his friend. I explained to Steven that I had found a lot of his belongings in the garage and put them back in his house. The papers and trash that to me was of absolutely no value had some importance to Todd? I couldn't imagine.

Then my nephew told me not to worry, and that it was trash! I loved him for being on my side. The next Monday, for some reason, I needed again to get into that garage, and to my surprise Todd had purchased a new lock! I asked Steven, "Isn't this your house?"

He said with such dignity, "There's more ways than one to skin a cat."

It was that day I learned to break and enter with a credit card.

Another Monday, I was vacuuming the sofa, and as I turned the cushions over, boing! There was a spring popping out, and again the boys blamed each other. Several days later, I called Steven on his cell phone and met him again in the uptown alley. I gave him no explanation, only that I had a surprise for him. Steven asked no questions. Leaving his friends, he jumped into my car and trusted I knew best. We shared enjoyment that day as he picked out the type and color of his new, no-boing sofa. I then drove him back to his friends.

It was now winter, and things were looking pretty good at 260 Wayne Avenue. While shopping at the Big Lots store, I bought the boys a skinny Christmas tree full of lights and some of Steven's favorite blue bulbs. I knew they both could use new socks, some toiletries and a tee shirt or two. I even found a big chew with a bow on it for Razz. I must admit the little white cottage home was shaping up quite nice. There were times when I'd be out and about in the evening, and before returning home, I'd make a point of driving down Wayne Avenue. I just wanted to see the skinny twinkling tree and the white candles shining through Steven's windows. The wooden snowman would be smiling as he waved from the porch. I couldn't wait until Monday.

It wasn't long after Christmas that Todd unexpectedly moved out with no goodbyes. I could see Steven's hurt and also a concern for the utilities. "Don't worry, you'll be fine," I told Steven. It wasn't until later I would come to understand there was good reason for his concern. For months a lot of mail lay unopened. I took it to be junk mail. Not wanting to throw it away, I filled a little Christmas bag and then another. After both bags were bulging I decided to take them home and go through these closed envelopes. I was shocked to learn Steven was deeply in debt to credit cards, his house was in foreclosure and his truck payments were behind. I asked him if he knew he was in trouble, bad trouble? He said yes. I was never as proud of him as I was that day when we fearfully grabbed up all the bills, climbed into my car and drove to a lawyer. We asked if there was hope. Yielding to the lawyer's wisdom and guidance to help free us from bankruptcy, Steven signed his money matters over to me, and my responsibility I gave to him. We had some sort of strength between ourselves that made us good for each other. I guess you could say we were of the same lineage.

Steven had not always lived on Wayne Avenue. His life had been to serve in the air force while furthering his education. Because of a tragedy, his dreams ended. Stevens' fiancée was shot and killed, and he then was severely hurt from a blow to the head, so severely that the air force disconnected him from working and the military. He and his grandmother tried desperately to get him reinstated, but the air force did not want to take the chance on his health ever worsening, causing his pension to be affected. Coming home, Steven did well, but as the years passed, it became harder and harder for him to find purpose. Alcohol became a close friend, and leeches of a human sort hung around, knowing his pension payday. Steven with a soft heart had become too vulnerable, and now we had this mission that seemed impossible.

Returning from the lawyer, we started to call the creditors. "You owe four thousand dollars, but if you pay today, it will only be seventeen hundred." That was one of the many voices on the other end of the phone. As we sat in his living room, I took out my credit cards, and in call after call, I maxed them out. But they covered less than half the true amount of debt. Steven didn't even flinch when they came and took his handsome truck. He knew it was the right thing to do. He bought a nice Nissan for nine hundred dollars, and we paid cash. It took five months to save the house. We had to change banks and use his father's name for good credit. When the Wells Fargo certificate came showing back debts were all cleared and payments were up to date, we framed it and hung it on his wall.

As I was looking at his bank statements one day, I ask Steven what all the thirty-seven dollar charges over and over were? Steven assured me they were overdraft charges. I then wondered why they never came and put him in jail. I then figured it out. As we were driving downtown one day and passing the grandest bank, I ask Steven if he liked it. Looking at me strangely, he said yes. "Good," I said, "because you paid for the left wing with all your thirty-seven-dollar overdrafts." He agreed.

In time even the checkbook was balanced. The lawyer was amazed how we did it. Me too. Inch by inch, we were climbing out of a Grand Canyon of a hole. Steven now was on a very fixed income and I was putting a kink in his drinking habit. He put me in charge and we couldn't turn back now. The leeches hated me. Even Steven's nerves grew thin at one point when he wanted more drinking money and I said no. Before he went out the door, he turned to his aunt and apologized. That was the only hardship we had and it lasted for only seconds.

One of our finest times came on a sweet, warm summer Monday. The yard was all mowed, and the house was spic-and-span. With the front door open, a cool, soft breeze often found its way in. I saw Steven turn the TV on and sit down to watch a movie. I had been busy in the kitchen, but I came in and curled up at the end of the new blue sofa.

We both were excited to watch *Spider-Man*, and I learned something that day. I learned Spider-Man's real name was Peter Parker, that he was a young man with many odds against him, but that he was still willing and ready to help others. I learned of his heartbreak, the loss of someone very dear to him. It was on this day that I saw the impact love can have on another. Wanting to do right together and having the power that grew to get the job done, two hearts could stumble through hardships, having not much, but having each other. Love always finds a way.

I did not know that Steven would soon be gone and that the alcohol would steal years from his precious life—a young, handsome man, age thirty-seven, a man that held a kindness few bear, a man of great character that wanted things right, a man that if he set his mind to it could do a work that was astronomical. That is who he was, and that is what he did.

-10-

One Year Later

It was October 23, 2006. I was sitting in an Indiana church with my children when my cell phone vibrated. Seeing it was Steven's cousin Tammy, I immediately left the service and called her back. She was sobbing as she asked me to pray for Steven. His family was afraid he was going to die.

The filth of the alcohol had won its battle. Steven slipped away that night, leaving many broken hearts behind—hearts that loved and would miss him in a way that would make it difficult to function without him. I knew Steven was now with God, because I had been in church when Steven walked an aisle and asked God to forgive his sins. Steven then trusted and in Jesus to get him to heaven someday. Today was that day.

I saw Steven's life change. I knew he was sincere in his prayer, but through the years and his hardships, I began to question his salvation because of his lifestyle. He sometimes scared me. I often thought I couldn't bear it if he didn't go to heaven.

During one of those cleaning days, he and I were back in the garage, throwing trash away. I just had to be sure and asked him one more time. Kind of kidding, but being firm, I said, "Steven, you get in this car right now with me."

Obedient as he always was, this thirty-seven-year-old man listened to his bossy aunt and graciously slipped into my car. Together we went through that old King James Bible and read each verse that clearly explained how to be sure you will be in heaven someday. I then explained to him how serious it was. It was his drinking that scared me, and the way he could never get victory over it.

"I did all of that, Aunt Cherie," he assured me again. As I looked straight into his eyes, I could, in some way, believe he was again telling me the truth.

At that moment, I knew for a fact that the eyes are the windows of our souls. Steven's words were not enough to convince me he was safe concerning heaven, so God in his grace showed me the window to Steven's heart. The path I was shown was so bright that I witnessed his peace, and then I could believe his words were true.

Steven experienced great loss, and when one loves deeply, one hurts deeply. The love of his life and his life's profession in the military had both been lost forever. Always loving, Steven had gentleness, peace, joy, and even the long-suffering that comes from doing right. These were gifts of God's Spirit, but there was one missing. I don't know for sure why—maybe because of his loss, low self-esteem, or inability to see purpose—but for some reason hope let go. Without hope, direction can become confused. That it did, but it didn't take away the Light.

The light of the body is the eye; therefore
when thine eye is single, thy whole body is
also full of light. (Matt. 6:22)

Steven's life was no longer in a safe place, and the hurts were winning ground. God wants his children well cared for, and there are times he calls us home because we are not doing well at keeping our souls safe. Only now can I look back and not wonder. God loves everything to be decent and in order. We didn't know it, but God was packing Steven's bags to leave. He wanted everything to look nice when Steven left earth: his home, his finances, and his debts, Steven owed no man. Every month a part of his military check paid for debts due, and in the end he had a little left over for his mother and father.

God's Spirit had moved in a miraculous way and with great purpose—for a departing. The songs had purpose, my going to the bar was for a purpose, Todd's leaving was for a purpose. Even the dog dying later that year, apparently for no reason, had purpose. The bills were in order and all paid for a purpose. One lawyer had all the counsel we needed for a purpose.

Although we look through a glass darkly and there are still some questions, someday it will be revealed. Trusting in God and doing right not only made the way possible, but became a journey to behold.

Owe no man any thing, but to love one
another. (Rom. 13:8)

Steven understands why now. He has all the answers. I have read of a great multitude that waits beyond the eastern gate of heaven. It will not surprise me, as I approach those gates of pearl, that there may be a little movement in the crowd as one makes his way through, someone a little taller than most. Even from afar, I will recognize him by those eyes that looked into mine many years ago and assured me he would be there. Words will not be important then, if we can just hold on to each other's hands, turn to the Son of God, and thank him for the songs, for the mission of order, for a year together that became a magnificent adventure.

The Eastern Gate

I will meet you just inside the Eastern
  Gate, over there
Oh, the joys of that glad meeting, with the
  saints who for us wait
What a blessed, happy meeting, just inside
  the Eastern Gate over there.
                                    —Isaiah G. Martin

-11-

My Nephew Steven: A Purpose

God gave me an essay, and Steven's story paved the way to my final story and the end of my writing class. Steven affected many hearts with his life and his death. He surely did mine. I was amazed how the professor and my classmates responded to his story. They loved him. They wanted many questions answered. I can see there was good reason, because I omitted the songs and the influence of God in the original submission. I was obeying the laws of the land. Even the professor wondered if I might be leaving out important information.

So with you, dear reader, I did as they asked. The songs are now here and so is God. I wondered in the beginning if I could ever bring together five pages of thoughts. After the touch of God to my pen, Steven's story could flow on and on. Little did I know it would become a stepping-stone to one more essay.

God has always been very kind to me. He, in all his mystery, would now, instead of opening the glass doors of opportunity and knowledge, opened a new set of doors. These doors would be the doors to my heart. No longer would we travel incognito. Instead, a veil would fall to the purpose of his will and to the laws of his land. "If it is his will, then let it be so."

> *If you can't see His way past the tears, trust His heart.*
>
> —C. H. Spurgeon

Sometimes I'm standing in line at a store or at a carnival and I'll see little boys dressed as Spider-Man. I whisper to them, "Do you know who Peter Parker is?"

To my surprise, some say, "No."

I then whisper to them before I leave, "Peter Parker is Spider-Man, I learned that with a boy such as you. His name was Steven."

With great power comes great responsibility —SpiderMan's
Uncle Ben

-12-

A Stumbling Block

Stumbling block: a block, stump, or anything else which causes one to stumble. 2. An obstacle of hindrance to progress, belief, etc.

At first I paid little attention to the fluid I was retaining in my left leg. I thought it was probably the result of too much salt in my diet and would soon go away. I was invited to my neighbor's for a jewelry party. I could see while getting ready that my legs didn't match. The normal one exposed the condition of the swollen one. I was wearing a long skirt, and I was sure no one would notice.

As I was standing at a table, shopping, my neighbor said, "What is wrong with your leg?" Looking down, I could see my ankle was now the same size as the upper part of my swollen leg. I told her I wasn't sure what was going on with this leg of mine.

A few days later, while visiting my stepdad, I asked him to look at my leg. Mr. Health, an advocate of flaxseed oil, wheat germ and special air purifiers, said, "I guess it is swollen.

You need to get that looked at." He kept reminding me of his concern throughout my visit. It was then I knew I had to go to a doctor.

Family Doctor

Visiting my family doctor ruled out a lot of things. He ended up sending me over to the hospital for a sonogram to confirm or rule out a blood clot. I had my clothes packed in the car. If the hospital released me, I was on my way to Indiana to see my children and grandbabies.

I'm not one to be sick, and fear of the unknown was lurking. I climbed onto the crisp white sheets and lay there as jelly was smeared on my enormous, unbendable leg. A nice technician carefully looked for a problem. I stayed quiet so as not to interfere with the images or the *blurp* sound coming from the machine. "So far nothing," he said. I think he knew I was a little out of my comfort zone. Upon finishing, he gave me the seal of approval and told me if there was the smallest of doubt in my examination, he wouldn't have let me leave the room. I now felt safe and secure as I putt-putted off to Indiana.

As I continued my writing classes, this leg began to have an assignment of its own—to give me fits. And that it did. Some thought these problems came from a bad fall I'd had at Christmas, but I had fallen on my head, and it was my leg that was hurting. All I knew was I did not have time to be dealing with a health issue now.

Dr. Hogue
Contact Reflex Analysis
Autonomic Response Testing

I remembered that through the years, a lot of my friends had gone to a highly recommended holistic chiropractor. They all had great results when dealing with their severe, out-of-the-ordinary ailments. I now was juggling college and my visits to his office. He seemed to be helping me, and I knew I'd be better soon. The swelling went down after six visits.

Then the symptoms reappeared; the swelling was back. Holding tiny glass bottles and touching parts of my body the doctor came up with a diagnosis: fear and dread. "What does that mean?" I asked. He didn't know. After exhausting every test and digging into my medical background, he suggested I get an MRI.

He might not have healed my leg, but he did a great deal for my writing morale with his interest and suggestions. My time there was not in vain. The words *fear* and *dread* were added to the concern of my sugarplums.

He released me from his care. Before I left, he asked what I thought the problem might be. I could see he wasn't shocked by my answer: "I either have something very seriously wrong, and the MRI will let me know what it is, or it's the devil wanting me to quit."

Dr. Ian Alexander
Orthopedic Surgeon of North Central Ohio

I recruited a fine orthopedic surgeon who ruled out some things and ordered an MRI from the tip of my toes to the top of my chest. As he filled his handheld computer with pages of information, I could see he too was stumped by my condition.

My leg was confined to one of those big plastic boots, although I didn't wear it to school. Hating it as I did, I must admit that it did keep the swelling down. There were days I had to stand against the wall in class, just to get circulation going so the leg wouldn't hurt so badly. Other days I wasn't sure I would make it to the classroom door without my leg bursting. I loved going to school, and I loved what I was learning. I developed a bulldog determination that I was not going to quit.

Physical Therapy

The orthopedic doctor sent me to physical therapy. The therapist took one look at my leg and wouldn't touch me, even though I had a slip for an eight-week course of treatment. He advised me to see an internist and heart doctor. Next stop!

Dr. Stephen Dean
OSU Heart and Vascular Center

One of the best doctors in Ohio wrote me up for more blood tests and more MRIs. I told him and his nurses that I would probably die of radiation poisoning before they found my problem. The nurses assured me I was safe. Dr. Dean prescribed water pills to help me walk more comfortably. He hoped I'd be able to bend my leg more. Before I left the office, the doctor told me that in some cases, they never did find the problem.

I was hoping the water pills would be my cure, and they were—for two days. As the swelling returned, it went into my right leg also.

As if that weren't enough, while I was cleaning the kitchen with a push mop, my left foot slipped on the wet rug. I thought I heard and felt a snap. It was so slight that I thought little of it. But the next morning, my left leg was swollen even more and black from my knee to my toes. I looked as though a train had hit me.

Calling Dr. Dean for a second appointment, I explained I had another complication with my leg. Soon I was sitting on his examining table for the second time. The doctor walked in, took one look, and exclaimed, "What happened to you?" I explained about the rug and mop. All he could say was, "This is bizarre." He had never seen anything like me.

He picked up the phone, called the orthopedic muscular doctor, and said I would be coming straight over. That I did.

Dr. Ian Alexander Again

I sat and waited again on another examining table. All my legs could do was hurt. I promised myself that from this time forward, I would always sympathize with truly sick people.

The door opened, and in came Dr. Alexander again. I could see he was shocked by the deterioration in my condition. I could also sense by the way he and the nurse looked at me that I wasn't their normal, run-of-the-mill patient.

Dr. Alexander thought that when my foot slipped on the rug, a muscle broke, and my swollen leg was now filling up with blood. "If this is the case," he said, "it will heal in time."

After four or five visits and another MRI, there was still no answer to what was going on with my legs. The doctor then decided to send me to his friend in Akron, Ohio, for another opinion, and I agreed.

Akron, Ohio

Believing my leg now had a hope of recovering, I made a date with a friend in Akron for lunch, scheduling it for after I visited Dr. Alexander's friend. Donna Kafka knew exactly where to meet me, and we were both excited; we hadn't seen each other for a long time.

"Do you need some help getting up, dear?" the sweet nurse asked me. I was again on crisp sheets, waiting for the door to open. In came another white-jacketed doctor. I wasn't informed as to his specialty, and wondered what he would say.

He took his time. The room was quiet. I was so tired of all of this. I said nothing. When he was finished, I just looked into his eyes.

"You're all right. You don't have cancer," he said.

I hadn't expected that. I'd had no idea that was why I was coming to this big city. I had mostly been thinking about lunch. I was speechless; you could have knocked me over with a feather.

The nurse helped me down from the table. I picked up my things and met Donna at the restaurant. We hugged, having not seen each other for a long time.

Before we were seated, she said, "How was your appointment? What did the doctor say?"

"Well, he said it isn't cancer."

Donna gasped. Cancer had been the furthest from either of our minds. Evidently it had been in the thoughts of Dr. Alexander.

Donna then asked me what I thought it could be. "Nothing," I told her. "I'm dying of nothing."

After our wonderful lunch, I putt-putted back home.

-13-

Final Prognosis

My final prognosis was that sometimes there are no answers, and my case was one of those times.

In the weeks to come, Dr. Alexander was proven right: the blackness did fade into a green and then yellow and became normal again. For months it was difficult to stoop, get up, wear shoes, or drive without becoming uncomfortable. Even though some swelling lingered off and on for eighteen months, I couldn't let go of hope. I didn't miss any classes to stay home and pamper this ailment like it wanted me to. I was afraid college for me would be a once-in-a-lifetime opportunity, and I so didn't want to miss it.

After all those months and now years, I often look back at that stumbling block, a hindrance that wanted me to quit. Many would say it was the devil. It might very well have been, wanting something less than the will of God for me. Although I think too of Jacob wrestling the angel of God all night, believing his opponent was an enemy. In the light of day, he saw it was not an enemy, but a friend. Then Jacob held on to the angel and wouldn't let him go until the angel blessed him. The angel changed his name from Jacob, the supplanter, to Israel, the prince with God. Jacob was told, "As a prince thou hast power with God and with men, and hast prevailed." (Gen. 32:24-29)

Sometimes when hard times come, we think they come from the Enemy, when they could very well be a lesson from God Almighty. Maybe my hardship of a dying leg was a divine struggle to see what it would take to make me quit.

> *Ye are of God, little children, and have overcome them: because greater is he that is in you, than he that is in the world.*
> —1 John 4:4

> *By perseverance the snail reached the ark.*
> —C. H. Spurgeon

Oracles of God's Storms

Essay 2

*I'm not afraid of storms, for I'm learning
how to sail my ship.*

—Louisa May Alcott

It was May 8, 1958—a normal spring day. At the age of seven,
I was sitting peacefully at my wood-top desk.

Cyclones are huge, revolving storms caused by winds
blowing around a central area of low atmospheric pressure.
In the Northern hemisphere, cyclones are called hurricanes or
typhoons and their winds blow in an anticlockwise circle. In
the Southern hemisphere these tropical storms are known as
cyclones, whose winds blow in a clockwise circle. Cyclones
develop over warm seas near the Equator. Air, heated by the
sun, rises very swiftly, which creates areas of very low pressure.
As warm air rises, it becomes loaded with moisture, which
condenses into massive thunderclouds. Cool air rushes in to fill
the void, and because of the constant turning of the earth on its
axis, the air is bent inward and spirals upwards with great force.

The swirling winds rotate faster and faster forming a huge circle, which has grown up to 2,000 kilometers across—that is 1,243 miles. In a category 5 status on the Saffir-Simpson Scale, these storms have been known to reach 190 mph. Countries and lives have been destroyed, costing billions of dollars to repair. One must be prepared for these tunnels of great current. In seconds there can be a loss of all power. These storms are deadly and very much to be feared.

http://creativecommons.org/licences/by-sa/3.01
https||Wikipedia.org/

A comparison of these hurricane and cyclonic storms to the emotional storms in a human's life may require more study. Then let it be so.

I was in third grade and today we had square-dancing lessons, I couldn't wait. I was hoping my partner would be Glenn Hammond. But first there were reading and arithmetic that had to be focused on. Class had just begun when there was a knock on our classroom door. "Quiet, class," said our teacher, Mrs. Sprang, as she lay her chalk down and left the addition problem unsolved. We all could see her talking very softly to someone outside the door.

When she returned it was neither to the chalk, nor the board. "Cherie, someone is here for you. You may go." I quickly put my pencils and papers away, and while walking down the row of desks, every step I took seemed so loud on the wooden floor. There must be something special going on somewhere, I thought, for me to be able to leave school in the middle of the day.

As I pushed the door open, there was my uncle Bill waiting. With a smile he said, "Let's go get Steve now. In the sixth grade, right?"

I said, "right." I was wondering what my brother was thinking as he was putting his things away, if he too thought this was something special to leave school in the middle of the day.

Then I could see my uncle had left his work. Whatever it was or wherever we were going, it had to be important. Steve jumped into the back seat, so I got the front. I sat practically on top of the windshield, my favorite place to see and hear all that was going on inside and outside the car. In those days they had neither a seat belt law nor seat belts.

As we drove out of the parking lot, I felt my brother and I both were wondering where this ride would take us. Uncle Bill was our mother's brother and such a kind person. As he spoke, he reminded us how our father had been sick for a long time. I then scooted from near the windshield to the back of my seat. It was then I realized why it was so important to leave school in the middle of the day. It wasn't anything like what I had been thinking it was; our father had passed away that day.

He had been sick for a long time. I remembered he spent many weeks on our sofa, with a drainage tube coming from his side. He had returned from a hospital in a big city that was somewhat far away, only to return to our nearby hospital. War had been hard on my dad. He had to be separated from a new bride, and because he had a gifted mind and a tender heart, the hurts of life had taken somewhat of a toll.

But all in all, if truth were told, it was the alcohol that killed my dad. It did soften the hurts that life so often threw his way, but it was also the culprit that murdered his liver and destroyed his pancreas. It was the alcohol that robbed my dad of his beautiful brown hair, and turned his chocolate eyes into a fog. A man five feet and six inches tall and 138 pounds had become very frail and was in much pain for a long time. He'd say, "Look here, sis, your arm's bigger than mine." I was his sis, and he and mom were the loves of my life.

Dad kept my brother and me in line. I remember being sent to the bedroom and missing a whole party one night. That was worse than being beaten for me. I loved being where the action was and had a tendency to be somewhat of a show-off. My father, knowing that, had picked the perfect punishment for my crime: separation from society. My dad had grown up in the generation that children were to be seen and not heard, especially during an adult gathering. He was right.

People said my father was ornery and that he was brilliant, calling a spade a spade. Many labeled him as kind and one that had compassion that made a difference. Being in a crowd, he drew a crowd. People wanted to be near him, and I had always been one of those people. As sick as he had been, I never imagined him being gone forever.

> May 8, 1958. In Loving Memory of Willis B. Cramer, 44, Perrysville, a native of Fredericksburg, died in Kettering Hospital in Loudonville, Wednesday after a long illness. A foreman and modeler in the mold department

at Manafield Sanitary Pottery in Perrrysville, he was one of the first persons employed by the pottery there. A son of Hiram and Mary Slutz Cramer, he was born Jan. 11, 1914. He came to the Perrysville community 25 years ago. He served in the air force in World War II. He attended Ohio University. He was a member of Fredricksburg Methodist Church, Perrysville VFW, and Lounonville American Legion. Surviving are his wife, Miriam, a son, Stephen, 11, and a daughter, Cherrie, (sic) 7, all at home; two sisters, Mrs. Lillis Musser of Akron, Mrs. Orrel Hosfield of Canton; three brothers, Claude, Logan, and Custer, all of Fredricksburg. Services will be Saturday at 2 p.m. at Perrysville Methodist Church. The Rev. Nils Johnson will officiate. Graveside services will be at Greenlawn Cemetery in charge of the VFW. Friends may call at Banks Funeral Home in Perrysville after 7 p.m. today (Thursday)

Wooster Ohio Daily Record

This was being read while I sat there looking at my father for the last time. It was as if he were sleeping beneath a blanket of flowers with an American flag near by. I knew with all my heart he didn't want to go away. I wanted to listen to what was being said, but at the same time a storm was brewing in my mind. It became more intense. I could feel a whirlwind going around and around within my confused mind: the fear of never seeing my dad again and the dread of wondering who would take care of my mom and my brother and me. It was this turbulence that drove my heart into the face of God. "Why did my dad have to leave?" I asked.

I knew there were others that lived as he had, and they were healthy and alive. I then asked again, "Has he done something really bad, God, that he had to go so soon?" As the storm hovered steadfastly within me I held back my tears and emotions. I could have even become bitter, I suppose, but it was then I heard God answer.

"You are not alone. I will be with you always even until the end of the world. I am a fear, a good fear to encourage you to do right. I do not come alone, dear child. I have brought with me a tremble."

I was very young to understand this quiet whisper. It was not what I wanted to hear nor share. Many would say I had imagined it.

With persistence, the voice went on to say, "Acquire this fear so you are always good and never hurt God, never make him angry in any way. But if you do, then tremble and get your bad right, right away."

It reminded me of the time my father became unhappy and I was sent to my room because I chose to be bad. I sensed my father, near and agreeing with every word this presence was speaking.

The others in the room were overwhelmed with their own hearts. My brother and cousins sitting near me seemed many miles away. I had the feeling my dad knew what was going on in my mind, and definitely God was involved with this tunneled force.

Then my mother's voice was calling me. It was time to go. I wondered what she would have thought of this still, small voice that haunted my mind. Jumping from my seat, I quickly tucked this conversation deeply away, onto the back burner of my heart, and life went on.

In the days and years to follow, if I strayed too far into a troubled area of life—you know, those places that hurt every parent— the fear of that storm would again haunt me in a protective way. It was always there to remind me of that day; the whisper in my mind warned me to be good and never hurt God. It was as though God and my dad were in cahoots. It wasn't a bad feeling; it was as though someone was always watching, someone that loved me a lot.

By June 1977, Mother had moved us to a quaint town called Bucyrus. I had been married for eight years and had a two-year-old daughter, Alana Loree. Life was good—that is, until another storm came.

Two weeks had passed since I had slept through the night. Fear and dread had new meaning now because of worry, stress, and tears that accompany them. I have always admired people that have a calm about them. You know, the ones that never raise their voices, and always have the right things to say because they know how to weigh their words. Their problems always seem to finish with a silver lining of contentment followed by peace. Some would say they take things with a grain of salt. How do they do that?

My family would often say I was too sensitive, or taking things too seriously. Until now, these dysfunctional happenings in my life had somehow found a way of ironing themselves out. This time was different. This happening started out as a category-five storm on the Saffir-Simpson scale of my emotions, and even then found a way to escalate.

Reaching out for help, I sought professional counsel several times, but peace had packed her bags and left me with no warning. Maybe I never really knew her? My own conscience had become an enemy, whispering from within that others were thinking the worst of me: slander, attack, gossip, hurt and heartbreak. There was nothing anyone could do that would remove the pain I was going through. My emotions had grown into a madness that resembled a storm that in time would tear me apart. I would be left mentally challenged, with no self-worth and absent hope, peace and any kind of happiness.

Friendship is having an attachment to a person with a favorable opinion, amiability, and respectable qualities of mind. It is a noble and virtuous attachment, springing from a pure source of respect, of great worth—a well-wisher, a patron, a supporter. Someone who knows the song in your heart and can sing it back to you when you have forgotten the words.

I no longer had a song in my heart and I could hear no one singing the forgotten words back to me. Why? I had lost a friend in a way that, even though out of my control, was in every way affecting my life. Many tried to comfort me and reason with my unstableness. I lost weight and became an empty shell, walking and pretending I was something I wasn't—all right.

Everyone has lost a friend at one time or another in life. Some people have no friends and they like it that way. Why couldn't I get past this and move on? Everyone wondered. I wondered. I went back to church, thinking that would heal me. I read my Bible every day and underlined passages that promised hope. Nothing was working, I could see others truly didn't see the severe effect this was having on me. It was like a nervous breakdown that wouldn't go away.

Every day I would go through the motions of a normal, happy person. After all, I had a lot to be thankful for: a family, home, friends, our health. But on this normal day while the sun shone, I felt I just couldn't go on. Laying Alana down for her afternoon nap, I went into our bathroom off our bedroom and knelt.

"Dear God, dear God," I prayed. "Things are so wrong in my life and I cannot find a way to fix them. My life has become unbearable. Am I doing something that makes you very unhappy? If so, God, I don't know what it is. Will you show me? Will you please fix it for me? Whatever it is, God, that you want today, I want to give it to you. I lay myself, my husband, and our daughter before you, I lay our home and our jobs over to you. I give you everything I have. I know you know best, and I know I can no longer go on this way. I feel so alone and abandoned, God. I beg you, please hear me, please don't turn your back on me. Please, dear God, I want to be the best I can, and I need you to help me. Forgive me for all my wrongdoings, and whatever is wrong in my life, God, will you please make it right. I love you so. Amen."

I was not familiar with the depths of God's Word, or the powerful truths he taught. Spiritual war zones, battles of right and wrong, and the value of a human soul were unfamiliar to me. For twenty-six years I trusted in good works to make God happy, and as I knelt in prayer, they had become as filthy rags. What did God want?

I did not know heaven and hell were choices of mine alone or that they both in a fighting manner had attached themselves to my ship of life, and neither wanted to let loose. It was I that had the final authority to choose which would go, and who would stay. It is this choosing that would determine my eternal destination.

Today had become the day of my salvation. I needed to release one or the other from clinging to the sides of my now sinking ship. The distress of this war-storm was ripping me apart and dragging my vessel under. Even though my vision was impaired, my emotions were in tune to this great battle. It was the storm of a lifetime that was raging to save a human soul from eternal damnation: mine.

These raging waves of influence had a purpose. God was using a happening (the loss of a friend) to get my attention. He wanted me to believe and trust in Him. Even though I was ignorant, God knew I was sincere in getting right. I had hoped for peaceful tomorrows, but instead lies and deception kept encouraging me to live on alone, without a Savior. I knew finally my peace must lie in something other than myself. If I must be a forever warrior of storms, I wanted to know I would be on the winning side. I did not want to ever again feel abandoned when crying out to my God.

It was on that sunny day in June that I surrendered all and repented of all my wrongdoings. God then introduced me to His Son, Jesus Christ, and it was He that saved me from the raging storm of sin and a real place called Hell. Because Heaven attached herself forever and a Spirit made Himself at home in my heart. It was He that calmed all my seas of emotion, and that day my burdens floated away into a foggy sea. Insanity no longer haunted me, and now heartaches of the day are their own destruction. I have learned when I am alone, I am not abandoned. It is in these times that thoughts of great victory come to mind, and I now live as never before. God's Spirit threw me a buoy and pulled me into the light of right. I'm so glad I trusted in Him and grabbed on. I could now see I had been too busy in life. Good works are good, but I needed Jesus to save me. I had been ignorant to the old, old story. God did not want my family or my home; it was my mind, my heart, and my soul he was fighting for.

My prayer became an invitation for God's Son to steer my ship. His map leads to a Wonderful Destination and His voyage is always a Magnificent Adventure. I wondered if my dad was not far away. My thoughts envisioned him with a healthy smile and a twinkling eye. I knew he would be happy with my choice. I knew he knew, and because of the coming of this storm, I now can call myself Christian.

Hold me fast let me stand,
In the hollow of Thy hand;
Keep me safe til the storm passes by
—Mosie Lister, Songwriter

There were many lessons I learned from this raging storm. Happiness comes from a happening, and when the happening ends, so can happiness. Joy is a melody that lives within the heart of a Christian always, and if subdued because of turmoil and sadness, this melody of love coincides with a peace that passes all understanding forever. It is God that sings back the words when you can no longer hear them. The puzzles of life He fits together so neatly and in order for a purpose. Every day there is the richness of an understanding knowledge and a gift of wisdom growing from his Word. Now I understand how some go through these storms and their end has a silver lining of peace. It's because of the Captain that is sailing their ship.

Many spend their whole life chasing their
own rainbows. It isn't until the end, if even
then they realize it has brought them to a
Diminished Future.
—Marie Neally

*The Lord hath his way in the whirlwind
and in the storm.*

(Nah. 1:3)

On April 2, 1982, everything went well in the delivery room, Adelle Joy Young was in the nursery, Alan had gone home for the night, and all the lights were now out. I and another lady lay in the same room, as we both had given birth that day at the Marion General Hospital. I could see she had already fallen asleep and thought it wise I do the same. Lying there quite still, I suddenly heard feet rushing down the quiet, darkened halls. Whispering voices penetrated my closed door. Then more feet were running, and I knew it was toward the nursery. One of the babies must be in danger. "Oh Father God, it is probably mine," I thought.

Our door then cracked opened just a bit. A soft-spoken nurse whispered so as not to disturb the lady beside me. "Mrs. Young, please come with me," she said.

I quickly slipped into my robe and slippers and followed her into the hall. Several doctors were waiting nearby and kindly informed me that our baby's heart had stopped while sleeping. Having revived her, they were going to prepare her for a life-flight to a nearby Children's Hospital.

Looking through the nursery glass window, I could see many doctors and nurses were working on this tiny human being of mine. More specialized physicians were coming down the hall. I was asked to step away as they continued to get Adelle ready for a helicopter ride. Not knowing where to go or what to do so not to disturb anyone, I turned the door handle to the nearest room and could see inside was a lot of big machinery covered with white sheets. The room was pitch-black but needed no light because of the windows that spread from wall to wall and floor to ceiling. Thousands upon thousands of stars shone from what seemed to be a black velvet sky. I had never seen anything so magnificent as being surrounded with such dark and such brilliance at the same time. I knew I was not alone.

Our home was forty minutes away, and even though it was April, we were in the middle of a terrible snowstorm. Alan wasn't sure he could get home and I wasn't sure anyone had notified him; our baby now was everyone's concern. I had signed a consent form, and many skilled doctors and nurses were doing a very important job: trying to save a life. I hadn't been missed as of yet and was in a room I'm sure wasn't one they were checking, a sterile machine-storage room.

Before I left I bowed my head and I prayed. "Dear God, I know I am not alone and you are here. I know your Son has the helm

of my ship. I can see plainly this storm is the worst I have
ever known. I wonder if I will survive, Father. I know there is
meaning and great purpose. I am not strong. I am weak, and
I beg you, Father, please don't let me miss the lesson of such
a horrific storm. If I must pass through this great turbulence,
please let me see as you and understand as you. Please let me
not miss this lesson, Lord God in Heaven. Amen."

The door then squeaked open and a nurse motioned me out
of a place I shouldn't have been. But in just a moment's time,
God had shown me his universe in the dark and in the bright.
He had again reminded me through his creation that I wasn't
alone. The nurse got in touch with Alan. Adelle had already
been flown away.

Adelle Joy Young was born April 2, 1982. She was diagnosed
as a trisomy 18 baby, which is also known today as Edwards
Syndrome. This is a congenital condition caused by an extra
chromosome. The number of babies born with trisomy 18 at
that time were 1 in 10,000, and the condition was usually fatal.
Today it is 1 in 6,000, and even though it is a very severe genetic
birth defect, some do survive and have quality of life.

Adelle did get to come home, and in that time, Alan, Alana (now
seven), and I took good care of her. She rode on the riding lawn
mower in a front papoose. She went to Alana's class events, and
Dad took his turn with rocking and changing diapers. Doctors
thought she may have a hard time eating, but we mastered
even cereal through an infant feeder, and eventually we all
learned how to tube feed our little baby girl. She never slept in
the night and for three months neither did her mother. When

Alan would go to work he would leave three girls on the sofa singing "Something Good Is Going to Happen Today." Alan would always smile and want to agree, but also reminded us not to get our hopes too high. It was hard to imagine, but I knew soon she would be gone.

Alan was working and Alana was in school. It was Grandma Young's turn to babysit while I had a doctor's appointment. I would return within the hour. I grabbed my purse and was getting ready to leave when Grandma Young asked me to come into Adelle's room. We both, looking into her brass bed, could see the angels had come in an instant and had taken her spirit home, so quickly that those angelic beings didn't even give her time to say good-bye. Whatever her mission on earth was, it came to an end after three months of her life. On June 30, 1982, our daughter was starting a new life beyond the clouds, way up high.

I knew I would someday see her again, but it seemed so long to me. I was thankful for my salvation and the storm of 1977 that drew me into a state of repentance. Maybe she and Steven both will be waiting for me. I never asked God why; I knew he wouldn't fix me to hurt me. There had to be a reason, but I didn't ask. I knew he knew best and I just trusted Him. Remembering the dark sky and the brightness of His stars I often reminded Him of my only request: "Please Father, don't let me miss this lesson."

Years later I would come to know the reasoning for this great storm. As for now, I held on to hope and continued to trust in the Almighty God of the black velvet sky.

I was driving three children to school in the year 1991. Alana was now fifteen, Hope was eight, and their brother Noah was 6. Seeing them enter the school doors, I continued on my way out of the parking lot. It was an exceptionally calm and beautiful morning. Many cumulus clouds crowded themselves close to the earth. I couldn't help but notice the beaming rays trying so hard to shine through the clouds, as if they had somewhere to go. It was as they were fighting to make their way to my steering wheel. These beams brought with them an emotion, a feeling of delight. I couldn't wait to get home and read the old King James Bible that, in these years of great storms, had become my closest and most loyal friend. God through these years had proven his love and faithfulness to me over and over as I opened my heart and trusted in him more and more. Little did I know this day He would reveal a secret and answer a prayer I had prayed nine years ago: "Please Father, don't let me miss this lesson."

Sitting at my kitchen table with a cup of coffee and my King James Bible, I came to the book of Deuteronomy, chapter 10, verse 16: "Circumcise therefore the foreskin of your heart, and be no more stiff-necked."

Circumcise has a spiritual significance in the Bible; it is referred to as a purification, an act of consecration to God. It is the cutting away of the hardened foreskin of a heart, the unkindness of resisting, murmuring, arguing, or disagreeing, leaving the heart sensitive to the Master's touch. In so doing, one can easily learn, understand, believe, trust, and accept God's way.

Cherie Young

Stiff-necked is quite the opposite. It is wanting my way and ignoring God's. It is the uncircumcised heart.

I couldn't help while reading, to think once again of those beaming rays trying to break through the clouds, as if trying to say something.

> *Arise, take thy journey, possess the land, fear the Lord thy God and walk in His ways. Love him, serve him, keep for thy good. Behold the heaven and the heaven of heavens is the Lord's thy God, the earth also. The Lord your God is God of gods and Lord of lords, a great God, mighty and terrible, which regardeth not persons, nor taketh reward. He executes judgment of the fatherless and the widow and loveth the stranger. Fear Him, cleave to Him and praise Him that has done these terrible things. And know ye this day: for I speak not with your children which have not known, and which have not seen the chastisement of the Lord your God, his greatness, his mighty hand and his stretched out arm. Never forget his miracles and his acts he did in Egypt. Hearken diligently to his commands. Take heed to yourselves that your hearts be not deceived, serve no other gods or his wrath will be kindled upon you. Lay up these words in your heart, teach them to your children, speaking of them*

when thou sittest in thine house, when thou walkest by the way, when thou liest down and risest up. Write them upon the doorposts of thine house and upon thy gates. Diligently keep my commands and walk in my ways, no man will be able to stand against you, fear and dread will be of you to them and I set before you a blessing if you obey and a curse if you will not obey my commands. It is my will that you pass over Jordan and possess the land of milk and honey. (Deu.10:11,12, 14, 17, 18, 20, 11:2, 3, 13, 16, 18, 19, 20, 22, 25 kjv.

These were God's commands to Moses for his people. A generation that was meant for a Promised Land chose to murmur and disobey instead and died in the wilderness.

After the death of Moses, Joshua was appointed and commanded to lead a new generation. God again knew their hearts and led them on dry ground through the Jordan to a place called Gilgal. God again voiced his desires through Joshua and knew their hearts could never minister to the level he desired. They could never conquer sin until their own hearts were first conquered. Joshua commanded them not to be as other nations but to step out in faith and identify themselves as the Lord's, renouncing their flesh and self-will. He encouraged them not to worry who their parents were that fell in the wilderness because of unbelief, but to remember they had been delivered from slavery, sin and rebellion. They were a people that was meant to be sanctified, guided and guarded by a Holy God.

Joshua, lifting up his eyes, then saw a man standing against him. It was this day Joshua met the Captain of the host of the Lord, God himself. The same orders that were given to Moses at the burning bush were now being given to a new generation in a place called Gilgal. It was a higher calling and a land of promise that was meant for his people. He told them uncircumcised hearts would surely defile this journey.

I knew this story was trying to teach me a lesson. Tears flowed down my cheeks. My shirt became drenched and the tissue box was now empty. It had become Such a Time as This. God was revealing to me why. It was serious; it was about the heart, a circumcised heart, and a journey. I trembled when I was sure. Deuteronomy over and over assured me of His desire that every heart be holy. I trembled wondering if this heart, once circumcised, could again become stiff-necked, self-willed, and leathered by an "I'll do it my way" attitude. The answer was yes.

Oh the price on these storms is so great, and all go through them. Even the ones that watch must endure turbulence. To travel in vain would be diminishing to a soul. I think of the value of these storms now that I have traveled them. I think of the ones that choose to ignore and never learn. I tremble and think of the words *dread* and *fear*.

A *testimony* is a good and solemn declaration or affirmation made for a purpose, establishing or proving some fact. It is a witness and evidence, a degree of light to the fact, affording meaning, an indication, and a statement of proof. A testimony can also be poor and irrelevant, of no probative value. Such a testimony does not prove any fact and is immaterial to the case, incompetent and meaningless.

Many years had passed since 1957, when I sat with my family in church but was alone with my mind while that healthy fear came in the mystery of a whisper encouraging me to always be good. The coming of the storm of 1977 drew me to repentance and the surrendering of my heart to God, as His Son became my Admiral and changed my direction of voyage, not only in life, but also for eternity. Then the great storm of 1982 taught me that even though my heart was saved from hell, every inner chamber needed much attention to live victorious.

Today it is 2016, and I am still sailing. I am still a student at arms. I know the sea of life will forever rage, and it is impossible to completely flee the waves of despair. But I have learned there is a safe place to go when passing through these angry storms. It is called the eye, a place of sure calm within the midst of these great storms. It is a region found in the center, twenty to forty miles in diameter, characterized by light winds and clear skies always. The cyclone's lowest barometric pressure occurs in the eye and can even be 15 percent lower than the atmospheric pressure outside the storm. It is here a peace that passes all understanding lives.

> *And my people shall dwell in a peaceable habitation, and in sure dwellings, and in quiet resting places. (Isa. 32:18)*

The eyewall is the complete opposite of the eye. It is a towering symmetric ring of thunderstorms, with winds and rain bands that spiral from the most severe storms of the world. Scientists do not have all the answers, but they do know that, for some reason, to have an eye of a storm, there must be an eyewall. They say without the eyewall, the eye cannot be formed.

Sad to say, there also is an eyewall replacement process. This occurs when an outer eyewall begins to intensify and contract. This forces the inner eyewall to weaken and eventually vanish, replaced by another eyewall. So the inner eye, the calm, cannot exist without turbulence.

These storms are the greatest forces known to man and should be feared by the world. Without these raging walls of wind, would there be a purpose for the protected learning of the calm? Would we ever have reason to hand our helm over to the sacred Admiral? The eyewall of life can bring one to a place of surrender and trusting that God will reach down and save.

Such great storm forces can be compared to the evil forces in our personal lives, the ones that tear our hearts to shreds, and are in the business of wrecking dreams as if there is nothing to live for. Only a change at the helm can turn a Diminishing Voyage into an Adventure of Magnificence.

> *Then they cry unto the Lord in their trouble, and he bringeth them out of their distresses. He maketh the storm a calm, so that the waves thereof are still. Then*

are they glad because they be quiet; so he bringeth them unto their desired haven. (Ps. 107:28-30)

Trust in the Lord will all your heart; and lean not unto thine own understanding. In all thy ways acknowledge him and he shall direct thy path. (Prov. 3:5-6)

-15-

My Cheerleaders

We were taught in English 268 that for a writer to continue, even the talented needed a form of encouragement. Their work is critiqued, criticized, rewritten, often omitted, and even rejected. All this is a part of the writing world, but having a cheerleader is too.

This is true in all walks of life, not just writing. Someone who encourages, believes in you, and is there to give you a push when you want to quit is crucial. It's one thing to have a desire and a dream, and it's another to have the grit, stamina, and self-confidence to make it come true.

I knew that with this last essay, I had stepped over the boundaries of rules. I was no longer incognito concerning my faith and beliefs. In so doing, I prepared myself for the worst: strong criticism and a poor grade. There were moments I thought I was happy with this last essay, and then there were times I could have permanently crippled myself with disappointment.

I came to school to learn, and that I did. Bob's conversation alone was filled with learning skills, and as I watched, read, and listened to the others, I knew I was in the midst of gifted students. I enjoyed our every second together. I practiced the art of faking it until I made it. Today it was my turn to be critiqued, and also it was the last day of our semester.

Entering the building, I stopped by the coffee shop and treated myself to a nice cup of coffee. While walking down the hall, I wondered what to put on my face so no one could see how nervous I was. I didn't know if I should smile or be serious. I kept the colorful, steaming cup close to my lips. Its warmth comforted me.

As I pulled my chair out, David Yoder came up to me, fanning my essay. He smiled and said, "You did it!" I knew he was referring to the number of pages. I smiled back at him. His kindness, mixed with a sincere funniness, blessed my heart.

Everyone took their seats. We sat in a large circle to listen carefully to all the thoughts and suggestions for making a better story. The one being critiqued said nothing, just listened and took notes about possible changes. All the students had in their hands a printout of my story. It had been their homework to have corrected it to its betterment.

The professor began. His criticism was constructive and true. Once again I learned. The students found most fault in the structure and grammar. Waiving the English class had returned to haunt me.

One young man, at the beginning of the semester, had made it very plain how he hated preachy essays. Today he pointed out that this story was not at all preachy! The teacher laughed a little and spoke up: "I believe the writer has found a way to go in the back door." Their tenderness and respect for my story was evident, and I loved them for that. Even Bob, as he pointed out mistakes and rewrites, had a sense of fellow feeling walking alongside him.

I had thought kindness was out of style and few wanted to wear it anymore. I was proven wrong that day. As I looked around the room, they all were dressed alike. I could see the months of writing had brought the solemnest of friendships. It was as if we had grown into a family and were now on common ground—the ground of higher learning, the ground of sharing hearts. I knew Steven's story had paved my way. He lived on in his testimony, helping my end be good. The clock was ticking as everyone handed me his or her corrections to my story.

I closed my folder and swallowed the last of my coffee. Whit Thompson stood up and started clapping. "Is he that glad it is the last day?" I thought. But then another student stood up, and another. The whole class was now standing in a circle, clapping for me. I was shocked! Bob and I tried to quiet them several times. He shut the door so as not to disturb the other classes.

I did not want to leave. It's a good feeling to be accepted, understood, and loved. I remembered Dave's words as I was leaving home that first day of school: "You go and enjoy yourself. You will learn from the students, and they will learn from you."

I can't speak for them, but I learned a lot. While handing in my papers and getting Bob's notes, I had to thank him for all he had done for me. It was his response that would remind me in the months and years to come to never give up: "I hope you know your writing is not meant to be just for your family. Since the beginning of this class, you have grown by leaps and bounds."

While driving home, I gazed at the sky and thought of all the doors God had opened for me during this time at college, Even though I had been afraid and unsure at times, I was glad I walked through each door and never turned back. I thought of my class reunion, the phone call, the high school transcripts, the nice secretary, the friendly admission man at the OSU office, and the gift of a scholarship.

I remembered finding my seat. While attendance was being taken, somehow I settled in. When it came time to write, I didn't know what to write. With a few words of encouragement from the teacher, "Who Is She?" and "Stardom" were born. Learning to use the computers and becoming friends with the students all fell into place. The coffee shop was a bonus. Sixty percent of my grade brought me to a place I didn't want to go, but took me to a place I needed to be. Then when the end was nearing, God used my classmates to encourage me to the utmost.

Tears came to my eyes as I laughed, thinking of all God's doings, Sitting behind the wheel of my car and driving down the road, I said out loud, "Thank you, God, for my professor and my cheerleaders. Will they ever know how much they have done for me and how much I love them? They are the best. You surely, surely made this a magnificent adventure."

"Iron sharpeneth iron; so a man sharpeneth the countenance of his friend".

-Prov. 27:15

Stay away from people who try to belittle your ambitions. Small people always do that but the really great make you feel that you too can become great.

—Mark Twain

-16-

Now What?

It would have been easy to stay on and continue with the next writing class, Creative Writing Fiction. The territory had become familiar and there was so much more I could have learned, but I knew it was not meant to be. I would miss the students I had learned from and the teacher I had leaned on for all my answers, but I could feel that abiding pull that was guiding me somewhere.

In the days that followed, I found myself jumping out of bed and making my way to a pencil and a pad, I had to quickly jot my thoughts down or they would fly away. "Are these scratches worth keeping?" I wondered.

I remembered Bob's words in school: "Never throw away a writer's thoughts, even if they're on a matchbook cover. They could become a book someday."

I could see these words that had robbed many hours of my sleep were fighting to stay alive. "Should they be heard?" I wondered. They wanted to be a parable, to speak allegorically. They were adventures, and my yes to travel with them is a journey.

An *adventure* is exciting travel. It can be risky and even dangerous, with an unknown outcome until you get there. A journey is also travel from one place to another. The best way to handle them both is to go. An allegory is a representation of an abstract or spiritual meaning through concrete or material forms, or figurative treatment of one subject under the guise of another.

"*There is something delicious about writing the first words of the story. You never quite know where they'll take you.*"

~Beatrix Potter (Author of, *The Tale of Peter Rabbit*).

"*Mine took me here.*"

-17-

The Lesson of Race

But the Lord said unto him, Go thy way;
for he is a chosen vessel unto me, to bear
my name before the Gentiles, and kings,
and the children of Israel; For I shall show
him how great things he must suffer for
my name's sake.

—*Acts 9:15–16*

My Horse

One of the most exciting days of my life was at age nine. I stood in our stone driveway, waiting to hear the engine of a truck coming down our road. It couldn't be just a truck, but a truck with a horse trailer behind. It wasn't long before I heard the shifting down of gears, and I knew there was a black stallion coming just for me. Mr. Rex, who was quite a horseman, was the hope I had. My mother totally trusted in his wisdom and judgment. My yells and screams brought my mom, my stepdad, and my brother out of the house. I could see their smiles and knew they were excited for me. At the same time, I'm sure my mother hoped I would be safe having my first horse.

The old truck pulled in, and a short cowboy of a man jumped out with a lead rope. He opened the back of the trailer. I could hear the sound of a horse's hooves trying to back out. "Come on, boy," Mr. Rex said.

And there he was, the most handsome black horse I had ever seen. Having some Shetland blood in him made his size perfect for me. Mr. Rex handed me the lead rope. I could hear him reassure my mother that this was a gentle horse and that I would be fine. I always rode the ponies at the fair, and I loved going to the riding ranges.

I suppose it was different to be on your own with such a large animal, and my mother did work every day. I could see why she might have feared what could happen to me at home and alone. I reassured her everything would be fine.

It wasn't long before Black Satin (I renamed him Nipper because he nipped) became a gelding. Being quit frisky for a beginner rider, this did calm him down a bit, but he was never slow or reserved. As for a barn, my mother always seemed to know what to do. Across the road was Wayne Erwin's horse farm. He just happened to have a building that wasn't being used and could be moved. It was the perfect size for one horse. Of course it wasn't as beautiful as the little white barn my neighbor Frances had for her paint pony, but I couldn't have been happier. Nipper was the most beautiful horse I could ever dream of having.

I learned quickly the relationship you can have with a horse, the amount of work they require, and the best friend they can become. It is said they require as much care for their spirits as for their physical selves. I believe this to be true.

Adventures come with owning horses, and I had a few of my own. I'll never forget the day Nipper and I tried to outrun a blue racer snake. I think we scared him, and he ended up running into a fencerow of weeds. While returning home one early evening from riding with Frances and Babe, I decided to cut through our neighbor's backyard. There was a row of hedges separating our homes, and normally I would ride to the back of the lot and go around them. As we galloped toward the hedge, I thought Nip would slow down. Instead, he accelerated and jumped the three-foot hedge. I had a crash course that evening on jumping and wondered where he learned that.

As fast as we could ride through many open fields, I was concerned what might happen if his foot hit a pothole. Fortunately we were always on sound ground. But once in the deep snow of winter, Nip fell to the ground with no warning, and rolled completely over. I managed to jump off in time, but the saddle went with him. Frances, riding with me that day, didn't know what to think. I think a roll in the snow looked refreshing to him. When he got back on his feet, I straightened my saddle and remounted, and off we went.

Probably the most exciting story of all was the summer day when everyone was working and I was home alone. I kept myself busy with yard work, housework, and horse work. There was always time, though, for *The One O'clock Movie* and *Jane Wyman Presents.* On this particular day, when all my work was done, I spent a couple hours with John Wayne. He and the

good guys were on horseback and running fiercely after the
bad guys. Coming to a river, the bad and good all jumped and
swam to the other side. I noticed how easy it was for their horses
to swim. It didn't take long for John Wayne to capture the bad
guys. The movie ended.

Getting up from the sofa, I wondered for a moment. The house
was clean and the yard was mowed, so I went to the barn to
tend to Nipper and put him in for the night. Our home sat on the
edge of a reservoir. There were still several hours of daylight
left. I wondered about those swimming horses.

Leaving the saddle behind, I thought maybe I'd take a quick
ride bareback. We didn't cross the road to go into the woods.
Instead, Nipper and I ventured over the hill and into the pines
near the reservoir. We didn't stampede or jump off a cliff,
though there was one there. We walked slowly into the shallow
water and stood for a while. Nip seemed calm, so we walked
a little deeper. After he got his fill of water, I kicked his sides
softly to send him out a little farther. I could feel his legs
swimming. Sure enough, we were on our way. I thought we
wouldn't sink, but I wasn't sure. He didn't seem the least bit
afraid and he wasn't struggling. He acted just like the movie-
star horses.

Nip jumped onto the bank on the other side. I was never so
proud of him as I was that day. Laughing and hugging him, I
looked into his eyes. He gazed right back as if to say, "Did you
think I couldn't do it?" I sat down to calm myself and let Nip
eat the high grass. I wasn't sure how long a horse should rest
after such a swim.

After a while, I asked him if he thought we could swim back. I jumped onto his back and he took me home. We too overcame the bad guys that day: uncertainty, fear, and stupidity were their names. Nip got extra hay and grain as I brushed his coat and rubbed him down. He knew why I was hugging him, kissing his nose, and laughing a lot. He knew he was a star! It was quite an adventurous day for us both.

We decided not to tell anyone for ten years. I knew then my mother's heart could take it.

When I stepped off the bus from school, my welcome would always be a whinny coming from the barn. It would often be dark when I was spreading new straw after riding. I was often in the saddle when my nose should have been in a schoolbook. This solace and joy I could not find anywhere except on the back of my horse,—the trails we discovered together, the luxury of having him, and him wanting to go wherever I led him. This was a friend who was hard to beat. To this day, one of the sweetest perfumes to me is the smell of a well-kept horse barn.

"You thought you would be fine, and you were," were my mother's words many years after I told her of my day with John Wayne. I wasn't 100 percent sure.

Thoroughbred Race

> *"It was believed that horses required as much care for their spirits as for their physical*

*selves, and that sweet temperament could
be absorbed like heat through the skin."*
-Nan Mooney, Author of, My Racing Heart

Byerley Turk, Darley Arabian, and Godolphin Barb, because
of these three stallions that made their way across the English
Channel in the sixteen and seventeen hundreds, there came a
breed and a linage of grandeur and speed. A true bred example
whether racing at the Sha Tin racecourse in Hong Kong; Prairie
Downs, Iowa; or the Ketucky Derby must have a linage tracing
back to one of these three stallions. Even though different in
size, color and personality these horses are all similar because
of their heritage. Their hearts being much bigger, ranging from
nine to fourteen pounds and an even more tantalizing quality of
this breed is their blood, it being thick with more hemoglobin
than any other breed, not just mythically but literally hot, the
large heart pumping more oxygen and swelling the red blood cell
count far above the many other horses known as warm blooded
breeds. Although these horses are well known for show jumping,
dressage polo, fox hunting, combined training and breeding,
Nan Moony in her book, My Racing Heart, has enlightened
the passionate world of thoroughbreds and their journey of
race. They were born with a purpose. They come from a grand
lineage. These animals are most at home when on a racetrack.
Their direction and purpose is not only to finish, but to win.

I couldn't help but relate what I was learning about racehorses
to the Christian life. There was quite a similarity. Thoroughbred
racing is a serious profession. It is costly and requires a lot of
training and endurance. Being familiar with horses is one thing;
being wise to thoroughbred racing is another. Likewise, being a

Christian is one thing; living the victorious, race-winning life is another. It is an allegorical parable, a life-changing lesson, but is it teachable? This story held a depth, a hidden spiritual lesson. Only in time would I see and understand.

It all started with an interview I was watching on a Sunday afternoon. Roy and Gretchen Jackson and their horse, the renowned Kentucky Derby winner, Barbaro. It was their compassion that drew me, and in my life it surely has made a difference

> *"And of some having compassion making a difference".*
>
> ~Jude 22

Delaware Park
Wilmington, Delaware
October 4, 2005

Delaware Park racetrack is a turf (grass) course often used by newcomers or horses that have not won a race. Winning your first race by seven lengths makes spectators sit up and take notice.

"This could be a good one!" the track announcer exclaimed as Barbaro went through the finish line.

Laurel Park
Laurel, Maryland
November 19, 2005

Six and a half weeks later, Barbaro was in a race known as the Laurel Futurity Stakes in Maryland. This is one of the richest and most important turf races held annually in November for two-year-old American thoroughbreds. Barbaro's speed took him eight lengths ahead of second-place Diabolical when he crossed the finish line. Once again, Barbaro captured the attention of the track announcer, who shouted from the box, "Wow, this newcomer is no longer a stranger to the racetrack. It is plain to see he wants to win."

The most sought-after jockeys ride as many as nine races a day, six days a week. While riding so often and on so many horses, it would be impossible to get attached to one horse, and I could see that was best.

After the Laurel Futurity, Barbaro was moved to Florida for a race and switched jockeys. Jose Caraballo, an excellent jockey who rode Barbaro in his early wins, stayed north and Edgar Prado, just as good a jockey, went south to mount what he thought was an extraordinary specimen of a thoroughbred. He wanted to travel wherever Barbaro raced.

Calder Race Course
Miami, Florida
January 1, 2006

The Tropical Park Derby, in Miami, Florida, is another turf race. The crowd of spectators wondered how Barbaro would run with the new jockey. Barbaro, a joyful-humored animal, could become serious when the saddle was put on. This is not true of all thoroughbred horses.

Entering the gate can be a major problem for some horses, and having a bad start can make for a bad finish. These horses can become spooked for many reasons. The jockey's well-being is also at stake. But in Miami, peace was with Barbaro and his new jockey. The bell rang and the gate opened. Barbaro was running hard and a couple lengths behind the front-runner, Mr. Silver. Mr. Silver angled around the turn and was three lengths ahead. Barbaro began to move of his own accord. Another horse, Allsmart, was closing in. Barbaro's new jockey made a smooching noise and that's all it took. The track announcer could once again yell into his microphone, "Under the wire, Barbaro and Edgar Prado winning by four lengths!"

Gulfstream Park
Hallandale Beach, Florida
February 4, 2006

The Jacksons and their trainer decided to take Barbaro off turf and see how he ran on dirt. The Jacksons had an even bigger dream for their racehorse, and the only way to make their dream come true was to introduce Barbaro to dirt racing. Few horses can race on turf and dirt; they do well on either one or the other. Many wondered what would happen with Barbaro. The next races on dirt would tell the story.

Races like the Holy Bull Stakes are known as prep races, races that separate the men from the boys. They can lead to "The Most Exciting Two Minutes in Sports," the Kentucky Derby in Louisville, Kentucky. The Derby is followed by the Preakness Stakes in Baltimore, Maryland, and then the Belmont Stakes in Elmont, New York. These three races, if won, make up the US Triple Crown, the greatest accomplishment in thoroughbred racing. Only twelve horses in the history of racing have earned the Triple Crown, the first being Sir Barton in 1919 and the most recent being American Pharaoh in 2015. Secretariat is perhaps the most familiar, in 1973. She too transferred from turf to dirt.

Gulfstream Park was a longer track, covering two turns, and it had been raining all day. The jockeys can wear five to six pairs of goggles as the mud flies. It is not uncommon for a horse to act up in bad conditions. The owner may decide not to take a chance and scratch a horse from the race.

Coming out of the gate and running hard, Barbaro settled behind Doctor Decherd, a horse that had won a stakes race a month earlier. How would Barbaro adjust to the mud? It was amazing how his legs adapted to the new surface.

Flashy Bull was pressuring from the outside. Barbaro moved out and was a length ahead. Then he got distracted by the TV lights that hung from the finish line. Great Point came from behind and passed Doctor Decherd. Flashy Bull took aim at the front line. A crack of the whip and a vision of Great Point veering in snapped Barbaro back into focus. Then came the announcer's voice: "It's Barbaro coming under the line, three-quarters of a length in front of Great Point. This is Barbaro's fourth race without defeat and his first on dirt!"

Gulfstream Park
Hallandale Beach, Florida
April 1, 2006

The Florida Derby is another important Kentucky Derby prep race. Like the Holy Bull Stakes, it was run on a severely muddied track, as it had been raining all day.

Position in race means a lot. In this last race of the day, Barbaro only had one horse in front of him, making the mud less of a concern.

This race would be more rigorous. He was number 10 in an eleven-horse race, putting him on the outside. It would be easy to get stuck running the whole race wide of the rail. Getting caught in the traffic could push him to the back. All this was of great concern, but Barbaro had proven he could take mud in the face and endure bad conditions.

The gate opened well, but shockingly Barbaro stumbled, bumping into another horse. Remember, a bad start often determines the finish. Immediately correcting himself, Barbaro drove into second and was soon close to the rail. Though a lot of dirt was flying, he was in a good place. Coming into the backstretch with a quarter of a mile to the wire, Barbaro was neck and neck with Sharp Humor, fighting in and out for the lead.

Barbaro got ahead, only to become once again distracted by the bright TV lights. Sharp Humor pushed hard. But with a snap of the whip, they did it again. "Under the wire by the length of his head, Barbaro and Edgar Prado are the winners!"

Fans were cheering. Family and friends swarmed around the champion. Barbaro had again, as always, proved himself beyond worthy. Now he was on his way to the Kentucky Derby. Everyone knew he couldn't lose.

Churchill Downs
Louisville, Kentucky
May 6, 2006

The bugle had sounded. "My Old Kentucky Home" had been sung. As the horses filed onto the track, I knew everyone's eyes were on Barbaro, the contender of contenders. The beauty as the jockeys, dressed in similar garments but different colors and numbers, spoke their names and who they represented. I could feel the excitement and pride that filled the stands. Barbaro as a beginner had won. As he stumbled and got back into the race, he won, As he became distracted by the lights, he won. Slopping through mud instead of his familiar turf, he won.

Great horses had visited this Kentucky track, many champions in their own right, but today this guy named Barbaro seemed to stand out. He shone brightly at times like this.

Twenty thoroughbreds were gated and waiting. The bell rang and the gate opened. Barbaro, number 8, once again stumbled in the first stride, but as before, he quickly recovered and in no time was heading for the first turn. After three or four lengths of the rail, Barbaro was behind the front-runners, Sinister Minister and Keyed Entry.

He entered into the backstretch with three horses ahead. It is here where most horses fall behind because they become tired. Sweetnorthernsaint and Showing Up passed him by. Keyed Entry and Sinister Minister had ruled the race for a mile.

Coming around the far turn, Barbaro lowered his head. He was getting ready to take off. Sweetnorthernsaint fell away. Keyed Entry and Sinister Minister were passed. Barbaro rocketed from fourth place into the lead. He stalled for a moment until his jockey reassured him with a crack of the whip that the race was still on. What a sensation!

Their lead grew from four lengths to five. One hundred and sixty thousand fans were cheering, Barbaro was six and a half lengths ahead of a 30 to 1 shot named Bluegrass Cat. All the other horses were ten to twenty lengths behind!

"Crossing the finish line, Barbaro has the speed to keep on racing. Barbaro has won the Kentucky Derby!"

Thousands of fans cheered while standing in the midst of greatness. The jockey pointed to the champion. "I never had to touch him; I was just along for the ride," were the words of Edgar Prado that day. This margin of victory was the largest since 1946, when Triple Crown winner Assault took the Run for the Roses by eight lengths. Barbaro's win made him the sixth undefeated horse to ever win the Kentucky Derby.

It had been twenty-eight years since the Derby winner went on to the Preakness, the second of the Triple Crown races.

Pimlico Race Course
Baltimore, Maryland
May 20, 2006

The Preakness Stakes in Baltimore is the second race of the Triple Crown. Barbaro had the chance to become the first Triple Crown winner since 1978. He was running with the superstars of his sport.

Barbaro entered his gate peaceably, but there was another horse, by the name of Diabolical, that was having problems in gate nine. Often when this happens, the front gate is opened, so the horse as it enters feels less confined. When the horse is safely in, then both gates are latched. Barbaro, hearing the second click of the doors, thought it was time to go and broke through his gate and started running. This being very uncommon, the veterinarian who was stationed at the gate, after a thorough examination, gave permission for Barbaro to continue. In seconds, Barbaro was reloaded and ready to run.

The bell sounded and the gates opened. All nine horses broke evenly, having a good start. Barbaro ran well through the first hundred yards. The crowd cheered, seeing Barbaro was right in step with the race.

Then his speed declined. The horse was pulled out. His jockey jumped to the ground. Barbaro stood on only three legs, favoring his right rear. The crowd was completely silent. Every eye was fastened on the injured horse.

Bernardini crossed the finish line. The crowd stayed still out of respect for Barbaro. The track officials put a screen up to block the crowd's view while the doctors examined Barbaro's injury. A loud voice came from among the spectators: "Don't you put that horse down, not now." Every soul watching was thinking the same thing.

A Bad Report: Would He Survive the Night? Three main bones in Barbaro's right rear leg had literally shattered into twenty-seven pieces. His condition was life-threatening. Unlike other animals, a horse cannot survive in humane circumstances on three legs. A broken leg can lead to complications as the other legs attempt to bear the weight of the horse's body. Thoroughbred racehorses are bred for speed, not durability.

Barbaro was then transported to the New Bolton Center at the University of Pennsylvania Veterinary Hospital. En route, sheets had been draped on overpasses with messages saying how much he was loved and wishing him a speedy recovery. It was amazing to see how this one horse had touched so many lives—not only in the racing world, but all over the world.

New Bolton Center Equine Intensive Care Unit
The day after the race, a five-hour surgery was performed to stabilize Barbaro's leg enough to walk on. It was one of the most difficult equine surgeries. A stainless-steel plate was implanted with twenty-seven screws, a new technology originally designed for humans. Barbaro had a fifty-fifty chance of survival.

On June 13, his cast was replaced. Complications affected both hind legs. Also, an abscess had developed on his uninjured left foot, and he had a fever.

On July 1, a severe case of laminitis developed in the left hind hoof. Laminitis is a potentially life-threatening affliction that is common in horses who shift weight to one foot for extended periods to keep pressure off an injured foot. This resulted in the removal of 80 percent of his left rear hoof. Both rear legs were now in casts.

On August 8, the veterinarians determined that the bones in the broken right leg had fused. The coronary band (the area where the hoof grows) on the left leg appeared healthy and encouraging.

On August 15, Barbaro was allowed to graze outside. The fractured leg appeared almost completely fused.

On September 26, the left hind hoof was improving. Veterinarians estimated it needed six more months of growth.

On November 6, a milestone was reached when the cast on the injured leg was removed permanently and replaced with a splinted bandage. The laminitis showed no new problems.

On December 12, a press conference was held to announce good news. The bandage on the right leg had been removed.

By early January 2007, however, laminitis was in the left back hoof and had become the source of further complications.

On January 10, another setback occurred. A section of left hoof had to be removed and a cast reapplied to the right hind leg. Aggressive pain management was required.

By January 27, Barbaro had developed an abscess in his right hind foot. Additional surgery was performed to insert two steel pins into the healed bones of his injured back right leg. Laminitis had now attacked his front legs. He no longer could sustain weight on any legs.

These setbacks brought a sudden and tragic reversal of fortune. Barbaro was euthanized on January 27, at around 10:30 a.m., by the decision of his owners, Roy and Gretchen Jackson, who indicated his pain was no longer manageable. Barbaro was gone.

I fell in love a long time ago with this beautiful champion, but it wasn't until he became a patient that the love took full force.

—Gretchen Jackson

We could see over and over how this exceptional horse tried beyond measure.

—Dr. Dean Richardson (Barbaro's surgeon)

If this is what it takes to train a Kentucky Derby winner, then it is pretty darn easy.

—Michael Matz (trainer)

He is the best I have ever ridden.

—Peter Brette (assistant trainer)

It was the right decision, the right thing to do. We said all along that if it ever became too difficult for Barbaro, it would be time. At a moment like this, grief is the price to pay for love.

—Roy Jackson (Owners)

As for me, I'm glad I rode him. He was a once-in-a-lifetime teammate. I'm so glad I knew his face. I'm so glad I saw his good days -and his bad days, too. I believe God sent him down to try to show us something. He was a wonderful example of courage and grace.

—Edgar Prado
(Jockey and Author of My Guy Barbaro)

> *Why is light given to a man whose way is*
> *hid, and whom God hath hedged in?*
>   —Job 3:23

In times like this, we forget the cosmic conflict that surrounds us. We forget that God's reasoning has purpose. Marie Neally would often say to me, "When your faith runs out, tie a knot in hope and hold on." But there are times when faith runs out and hope is misplaced. We must then trust that God will give us a glimpse of himself, he who is invisible.

> *"Alas, my master! How shall we do?" And*
> *Elisha prayed, and said, "Lord, I pray thee,*
> *open his eyes, that he may see". And the*
> *Lord opened the eyes of the young man;*
> *and he saw: and behold the mountain was*
> *full of horses and chariots of fire round*
> *about Elisha. (11 Kings 6:15,17)*

Elisha's servant was fearful, seeing they were greatly outnumbered by the enemy—a situation of no hope. Elisha said, "Fear not for they that be with us are more than they that be with them" (11 Kings 6:16 kjv) As Elisha looked up and reached unto God, his servant's eyes were opened. He saw on the mountain a massive army of chariots of fire. Elisha and his servant envisioned the compassion and power of he who is invisible.

All the wise men of Babylon were going to be killed and their homes burned. This group included Daniel and his Hebrew friends Hananiah, Mishael, and Azariah, better known as,

Shadrach, Meshach and Abednego. Why was the king's decree so severe? He wanted to know the interpretation of a perplexing dream, a deep secret that his wise men and their gods could not reveal. Daniel and the three Hebrew men prayed to their almighty God that they would not perish with the others and the secret would become known.

Then Daniel went in, and desired of the king that he would give him time, and that he would shew the king the interpretation. Then Daniel went to his house, and made the thing known to Hananiah, Mishael, and Azariah, his companions. That they would desire mercies of the God of heaven concerning this secret. Then was the secret revealed unto Daniel in a night vision He revealed the deep and secret things: He knoweth what is in the darkness, and the light dwelleth with him.

> *"I thank thee, and praise thee, O thou God of my fathers, who hast given me wisdom and might, and hast made known unto me now what we desired of thee: for thou hast now made known unto us the king's matter." (Dan. 2:23)*

You may say in these two stories the champions lived, and that is true, but there is another story in which the greatest of all champions died. He came for a purpose, and in winning he lost. His death was not understood, but his love was contagious, and multitudes took on his attributes. Through others, he shines, and through life and death, he will always be to the heart, mind, and soul the champion, Jesus Christ.

Attributes are our inward belongings that profess our outward testimony. They are with us wherever we go, and we are known for and by them. They describe our character as honest, respectful, thankful, kind, truthful, self-controlled, obedient, and forgiving; or as disrespectful, unthankful, unkind, lying, prideful, grudging, larcenous, jealous, envious, and unforgiving. These are characteristics of our choosing and make us who we are.

Whom do men say that I am? (Mark 8:27)

He was a talent with a humble demeanor who nonetheless stood out in the crowd, a peculiar treasure with a winning spirit who had an uncommon intelligence alongside guts and bravery. I saw a pride that carried great accomplishments while living up to every expectation of honor. He never had to be told twice what to do, and many times did what was right before being told. Hearts were at attention as hundreds hung on a fence, thousands peered from the stands, and millions viewed from their homes. They all had one thing in common: a desire for the meek-spirited power under control to do what he had been called to do—win. The story became worldwide and captured the hearts of nations.

Barbaro loved to race. He loved who was on his back. He loved to work. He loved to play. Because of his love, he became contagious, and others around loved him right back. It is true in all walks of life: with such a personality, jealousy is sure to deter this kind of grandeur. It's inevitable. Maybe that's why these loving characters often walk a little higher than the clouds. It's not that they are better, but they escape the negative.

Getting mud in the face did not slow Barbaro down nor hurt his speed. He knew the rules. While hugging the rail or waiting for a hole, he never became intimidated. Instead, he intimidated. Again I could not help but apply this quality to the Christian life. A racehorse had accomplished something most Christians never do. His love was finding a way to win. Even though negativity beats at one's door daily, this beast was a grand example of pure endurance, far above the measure of normal. All his inward attributes professed a magnificent outward testimony in doing well.

So why did good turn out to be so bad? Elisha's fearful servant could not see the cosmic warriors around him, but because of prayer, they were revealed. Daniel and his three friends were at death's door. Once again, prayer saved them by interpreting the mystery of a dream.

> *I thank thee, and praise thee, O thou God of my fathers, who hast given me wisdom and might, and hast made known unto me now what we desired of thee: for thou hast now made known unto us the king's matter. (Dan. 2:23)*

> *"Lord I pray thee, open his eyes that he may see." And the Lord opened the eyes of the young man; and he saw. (2 Kings 6:17)*

A world of cheering went silent. Eyes focused on a proven and loyal vessel, a vessel that could not speak through victory that day at Pimlico. He would not charge under the wire; the announcer would not yell his name from the box with great volume and excitement.

What was going on in the cosmos? What would be seen if the spiritual surroundings became enlightened? I wondered. Millions of hearts lay in a melting pot as they looked upon what they saw as defeat. Through a life-threatening injury, could there be a message that wanted nothing more than to echo down through the ages?

I cannot speak for the ones on the fence, nor for the fans in the stands, nor even for the millions in their homes. I can only share the message of whisper that found its way into the pages of my heart.

My Dear Friend,

I will not run this race today. Therefore I will not thunder to get the Triple Crown. The Triple Crown is believed to be the greatest accomplishment for a three-year-old thoroughbred. I know many hopes were high. Great faith believed I was born and bred for stardom. I have been watched and rallied to success, being blessed to become a torrent of speed. I'm sure today you and many others feel let down, but I must say all has happened in the name of love.

The same power that made me win has handed me this microphone of injury. When the bell rang and the gate opened, I knew mysteriously and seriously that something happened.

My jockey knew because he knows me. When he pulled me off the track and jumped to the ground, I could see he was confused. His heart was immediately affected, as too was my trainer's and my owners' and yours.

I am grateful for the happiness and joy my life has brought to so many. You have been my friends. Thank you for believing in me. I know it is very difficult to understand, but what you see today is an even greater elation than a Triple Crown. The greatest race I have been chosen to win is the race of your heart.

> *For the Lord seeth not as man seeth; for man looketh on the outside appearance, the Lord looketh on the heart. (1 Sam. 16:7)*

> *But the Lord said unto him. "Go thy way: for he is a chosen vessel unto me, to bear my name before the Gentiles, and kings, and the children of Israel. For I will show him how great things he must suffer for my name's sake." (Acts 9:15-16)*

> *But in a great house there are not only vessels of gold and of silver, but also of wood and of earth; and some to honor, and some to dishonour. If a man therefore purge himself, he shall be a vessel unto honour, sanctified and meet for the master's use, and prepared unto every good work. (2 Tim. 2:20-21)*

While running a race, some start out well, but before the finish are overthrown. Some have honor, but in the run discouragement takes hold. Good must encourage more good while keeping its eyes turned toward even more good. Then good learns to reign. Bad often pushes. Integrity may let itself be pushed, but continues to stay sure-footed in obedience and perseverance. Standing firm in the rules brings sanctification and ordination for the Master's use. Because of great attributes, the Master sees plan and purpose.

> *And the evening and the morning were the fifth day. And God said, Let the earth bring forth the living creature after his kind, and it was so." And God made the beast of the earth after his kind and God saw that it was good. (Gen. 1:23-25)*

Could this race be pressing toward another mark? With such a heritage and a bloodline, was the cosmos in tune to a higher calling? Attributes are one's testimony. Laying aside every sin that besets one is a testimony to behold. Others are watching. Being fearful of doing wrong and teachable about the right—is this not the greatest of beginnings?

Truth sets one on the track of a great race. Love, being a champion of endurance, knows how to get mud in the face and survive being pushed to the rail. Love watches for a hole to excel and continues to always do right. Love has a peace that walks where few travel, above the clouds, escaping many darts of the enemy.

Know ye not that they which run in a race run all; but one receiveth the prize? So run that ye may obtain. And every man that striveth for the mastery is temperate in all things. Now they do it to obtain a corruptible crown; but we an Incorruptible. (1 Cor. 9:24-25)

Nay, in all these things we are more than conquerors through him that loved us. For I am persuaded, that neither death, nor life, nor angels, nor principalities, nor powers, nor things present, nor things to come, Nor height, nor depth, nor any other creature, shall be able to separate us from the love of God, which is in Christ Jesus our Lord.

And I saw heaven opened, and behold a white horse; and he that sat upon him was called Faithful and True. He hath on his vesture and on his thigh, a name written "King of Kings and Lord of Lords". (Ro. 8:37-39, Rev.19:11-16)

When trying to reach into the chambers of the human heart, love finds a way. There are lessons in life that only great suffering can teach. The greatest reward is the reward of no reward but the reward of knowing what you are doing is right. What you send out will in time come back. What goes around will come around.

In Barbaro's race of life, so much good was sent out. In the end how will all that good come back around? The race of a life time is to prepare our hearts for an incorruptible crown.

> *I believe God sent him down to try to show us something?*
> *He was a wonderful example of Courage and Grace.*
>
> —Edgar Prado

Revelation 19:11–16
Romans 8:37–38
Philippians 3:14
Revelation 19:11,16
John 14:6
James 1:12
Hebrews 12:1

-18-

Shine

It was December 2008, the bells were ringing and a light fall of snow was getting everyone in the Christmas spirit. I was in the attic digging through boxes and wondering how I could burn out every strand of fifty-count white lights at the same time. Not one working set could I find.

Oh, I hated the thought of having to quit in the middle of my jovial work and go to Walmart. Walmart is not a place one can run in and run out of—at least I can't. I have to look around a little. Then there are people you haven't seen for months, and we always have to catch up on each other. The checkout lines aren't too bad, but it's Christmas. I knew the parking lot would be packed. I hated walking in the wind. I just hated the thought of interrupting my festive digging so I could go to Walmart. But I did.

Trying hard not to look around, I went straight to the Christmas aisle. Glancing over every shelf, I could not see the fifty-count white lights. I found pink, blue, and even green, but nowhere did I see the white.

"May I help you, ma'am?"

I turned. There stood a friendly man whom I thought looked familiar. He had a face that I had known throughout my life, but not as a Walmart clerk.

"Yes, sir," I said. "Do you have any fifty-count white Christmas lights?"

Before I could finish my sentence, he scurried off. As quick as he left, he returned. He explained he could find only one box that a customer had bought by mistake and returned. "We are out of them now, but we will be getting some soon. You'll have to come back," he said.

My mission was in vain. I had to come back. "Great," I thought. I thanked him for his trouble and kindness and knew my Christmas decorating wasn't going to get done that day.

Before I left the concerned and friendly clerk, I ask him if he had retired. He laughed and said, "From which job?"

Many years had passed since the wooden chairs of the fire station were lined up on the sidewalk. It was quite impressive to see the firemen sitting outside on a summer day in their blue-and-white starched shirts with badges and patches on them. They were a friendly group, and one got the impression they enjoyed their occupation. I especially remembered one man because of his pleasant countenance. Also he had a different kind of name that forever stuck in my memory: Dallis Easterday.

That was where I remembered the Walmart clerk from; to me, he was that fireman of many years ago. He told me he had been retired from the fire station for eight years, and since then he had worn many hats. They were hats of honor, as I would learn later.

I left the store in good time but was not super happy with only one box of lights. The fireman-clerk was right; I would have to come back.

Walking to my car, I didn't mind the wind, and as I pulled away, I didn't even notice the congested parking lot. Instead I smiled as I thought of that pleasant fireman-clerk. Even though I couldn't finish what I was doing at home, the trip to Walmart and the freshness of the winter day seemed different this time. Was it the clerk? He couldn't fill my order; we didn't find what I needed. Yet I felt as though I was going home with something I hadn't come with. I just didn't know what it was.

A week later, there I was again, trying to find a parking space close to the Walmart door. I was hoping by now they would have those fifty-count white lights and my visit wouldn't again be in vain. While trying to pull out a shopping cart that didn't stick to all the others, I heard a loud shout coming from the center of the main aisle: "Hey! Hey, lady! Those fifty-count white lights, we got some in."

A man was waving, motioning me to come his way. It was my fireman-clerk friend. I couldn't believe he remembered me. He even remembered what I needed. Shocked and amazed,

I followed this cheery elf to the Christmas aisle. How had he known that was why I was there?

Just like before, he disappeared and reappeared. This time, his arms were filled with little green boxes. "How many do you need?" he asked, stacking them into my cart.

"I'll take them all," I told him, thinking I would not have to come back for a long, long time—at least not for fifty-count white lights. I could see the season was keeping him very busy, so with a smile, a Merry Christmas and a thank-you very much for all his help, I went on my merry way.

As I put my cart away, I was thinking again of his help and consideration. I thought maybe I shouldn't be so full of dread and weariness when coming to Walmart. Walking through the parking lot, I was happy to now have more than enough lights to finish my festive projects. But for some reason my mind kept going back to the arm-waving clerk yelling, "Hey, lady, fifty-count white lights."

I clicked my car locks open and got into my car. I laid the lights on the seat next to me. As I put the key into the ignition, my mind kept thinking of the fireman-clerk's attitude of service and armful of small green boxes. I wondered, "What is it, God? What was that? Wasn't he just a man in the Christmas aisle?" These thoughts lay heavy on my mind but at the same time would always be cheerful to me. I actually laughed out loud as I was pulling out of the lot. Whatever that was with the Christmas clerk, I wanted some of it.

Eight months later I opened the newspaper and thought, "It can't be." There was a picture of Dallis Easterday. He looked so handsome in his fireman's uniform, his hat tilted just a little down. That was exactly how I remembered him. Pulling a chair out and sitting down slowly, I couldn't believe what I was reading. Why would such a vibrant man die? As I read on, I understood what he had said to me about retirement: "From which job?" The list in his obituary went on and on about all his lots in life.

What a wonderful man I met that day in the Christmas aisle at Walmart. But then, I think I knew that. Sitting in my kitchen alone in the quiet of the day, I was saddened that I had only known him for such a short time. But in that short time, I thought of the impression he had made on me. He was a unique sort. I knew he would be greatly missed by many.

What was it that had made him stand out? That had made him extraordinary and unusual? Whatever it was, I wanted it. It not only made me smile, it made me laugh out loud. What was it, God? It was *shine*.

Yes, that was what it was. I should have known that. Now it was becoming clear. No wonder I loved it; no wonder Walmart was a better place because of it.

Immediately I thought of a song I had sung as a little child:

> *This little light of mine, I'm gonna let it shine,*
> *Shine all over the neighborhood, I'm gonna let it shine,*

> *Don't let Satan poof it out, I'm gonna let*
> *it shine,*
> *Let it shine, let it shine, let it shine.*
> —Harry Dixon Loes

I'm so grateful Dallis let his light shine so brightly. I'm grateful he did not limit it to just his good days. I might have missed those days, because we only met twice. I'm grateful he let his light shine not only in his home and with his family, but also in my neighborhood. That way, my and others' lives have been changed.

I'm grateful that Dallis did not let Satan poof out his shine. As silly as it may sound, it is profound and true. It is Satan's everyday job to poof out the shine in our world. When he does so, defeat prevails and shine can become extinct. It is not always easy to shine; it can even become a battle and a trial to preserve shine on a day-to-day basis. But a life that can preserve its shine is a victorious life.

Studying the word *shine*, I learned this type of person doesn't think it odd to serve others. It is not an inconvenience; in fact, they get great joy from doing so. They are quite rare birds and are becoming an endangered species. You know kindness is not in style. These birds wear it anyway, and how becoming kindness is on them.

Their smiles come from within, triggered by a fountain of inner joy. This can be contagious if you let it. That is what I experienced every time I came into contact with Dallis. On that day at my kitchen table, I determined to make a serious change in myself. Many may say I am a joyful and happy person, but what they don't know is at times I dance with depression, insecurity, and fear. I often get concerned about what others think. It often molds my behavior and limits my abilities. The woes of this world can bring a thick fog to the path of my day. Since I met Dallis Easterday, captain of the fire department and a gracious Walmart clerk, his countenance has made me want to become a better example of *shine*.

Dallis Easterday, Fireman

He attended schools in Bucyrus and
graduated in the class of 1961.
He was a US Army veteran, 1961–1964.
He worked for General Hydraulics and
Pittsburg Plate Glass.
He then joined the Bucyrus Fire
Department in 1971.
He became a lieutenant in 1977 and captain
in 1982.

Dallas graduated from Columbus State
College in 1984 receiving an associate's
degree in fire science.

Dallas was promoted to department chief
in 1986 and served in that role until he
retired in 1996.
Following his retirement, he continued his
love for Bucyrus by serving on the city
council from 1998 to 2005.
He also served as a Crawford County
commissioner from September 2000 to
January 2001.

Dallas did recycling.
He was a mentor at Lincoln Elementary
School.
He was a courier for the United Bank.
Most recently, he could be seen stocking
shelves, being a cashier, and helping
people at the Bucyrus Walmart.

Dallas attended the First Church of the Nazarene and was involved in many church activities, including coaching Upward Basketball.

—from the Bucyrus, Ohio, *Telegraph Forum* Obituaries

No wonder Dallis laughed when I ask if he had retired. He surely was a man of many honorable hats. I had known there was something special about that guy and now I knew what. What a privilege for me that our paths in life crossed. What an impact he made on me. I will never, never forget my friend who taught me through example the importance of *shine*.

Let your light so shine before men that they may see your good works, and glorify your Father, which is in heaven.

—Matthew 5:16

And of some have compassion, making a difference.

—Jude 22

Be ye followers of me, even as I also am of Christ.

—1 Corinthians 11:1

-19-

Shine, Part Two

It was July 19, 2009. I was excited to visit my grandchildren in Indiana. Putting the last few things in my suitcase, I knew the trip would be bittersweet. Dallis Easterday was being buried. He had only been sixty-six years old, and had passed away because of complications after a heart surgery. Although I had only met him on two occasions, it seemed we had been friends forever.

All I could do was drop a basket of goodies and a sympathy card by his home, and share with his wife how her husband had been such a blessing to me. They lived on Hopley Avenue, the same road that took me into town every day. For many years I had seen Dallis mowing his yard and enjoyed the way his wife decorated their porch for the different seasons.

As I pulled in, the drive took me around back to a small walkway that led to a beautiful sunroom. I could see the house was dark. Was no one at home? You can often tell a lot about a person when visiting their home. It didn't surprise me at all to feel a solace and welcome that needed no mat. Seeing everyone was gone, I put the basket in a protected area where his family would find it later. Though I was sorry to miss them, I knew I would meet them another time.

Driving through town, I took a side street to miss a lot of traffic. Stopping at the light in front of our library, I could see to the right that the fire station had two large fire trucks blocking the street. The truck ladders were extended, it seemed into the clouds, and were touching each other. Underneath the ladders I could see figures of people. Then I knew why the Easterday home had been dark and empty: the fire department was having a memorial for Dallis and his family.

What a coincidence that I had taken the side street instead of the main one. Now I had a memory of his memorial. What a sight, seeing these two big red engines with ladders to the sky, and his family beneath. I wondered what was being said. I knew there must be a lot of wonderful words about a good man.

As I was leaving our city limits, a soft rain began to trickle on my windshield. The sunny sky had turned to a charcoal gray as I got on the freeway for a five-hour trip. Memories comforted me for the friend who was gone. Alone in my car, I pondered my two short meetings with Dallis. It was the quality of a moment that kept teaching me metaphoric lessons during the quietness of my trip. Because of Dallis Easterday and his life, a secret was made known to me—the importance of a heavenly shine.

After having a wonderful time and returning from Indiana, I stopped by the Easterday home several more times, never catching anyone at home. On one occasion, I left a note of testimony, explaining how this man had been such a blessing to me. Months passed. I never met any of the Easterday family. Often as I passed their home, I hoped they were doing well.

Then came another Christmas season. I was excited to be invited to a ladies' Christmas gathering at church and even asked to give a devotional lesson. What could be more appropriate at Christmas time then to learn how to shine more brightly? I wrapped up little green boxes of fifty-count white lights in shining silver paper and silver bows. I surely had enough because of that great clerk who helped me to make the purchase.

I then made a booklet with an outline of the lesson. The pages were held together with a shining silver metal snowflake. I opened a cupboard drawer to put things away, and a box of Christmas cards caught my eye. On the front was a snow-covered pine tree glittering with sparkly flakes, bright in the midst of a dark blue night. The box had not been opened and probably was bought on sale for no reason other than its beauty. Well, it now had a reason for this season.

I had such fun preparing the lesson. I wanted the ladies to feel the joy and learn the importance of possessing *shine*. And guess what? They loved it all, especially the fireman-clerk who spread his shine to the world. I hoped they would never forget this evening and would always cherish what they had learned, forever passing their shine on.

Since it was Christmas, I made up one extra basket. In you go: one silver-wrapped box of fifty-count white lights, one card and booklet of the story, add a few sweets, and then finish it off with a big bow. Again no one came to the door at the Easterday home. This time I set the basket at the front door. I knew in time it would be found. It was just a thought to say, "Merry Christmas and blessings and love."

I began to wonder if Mrs. Easterday had been offended by the notes I left. Maybe I should have been more selective with the words I chose in writing about her husband? She might think I was a stalker and approached her husband in an inappropriate manner. "Aw, maybe I best back off," I thought. My motives were pure. I had met a wonderful person, and I knew he had to have a wonderful wife. I decided not to worry about the situation.

When I drove down Hopley Avenue again, it was Friday, my day to volunteer at the hospital gift shop, a place from which it was hard not to bring something home. We had many volunteers, and even though I had been working there for years, it was impossible to know everyone. The schedule listed us by first name only.

Today I was taking over from a name I wasn't familiar with, a lady named Fran. Sure enough, when I walked through the door at 12:30 p.m., I could see a woman waiting eagerly to be relieved from the register. As usual, the shop was buzzing with activity, and the bosses were busy decorating.

Fran looking directly at me and asked, "Are you the Cherie Young who keeps putting things at my door?"

I was speechless. I couldn't believe what I was hearing. "Are you Dallis Easterday's wife?" I asked.

Fran and I had never worked near each other. This was our first meeting.

I told her I had been trying to meet her for over a year. The buzzing of the gift shop became silent. All the decorating came to a halt. Everyone was in wonderment at what was going on.

Fran told me her children lived far away. She had shared my notes with them over the phone, but often her tears got in the way of the message, she said. I knew then she wasn't offended and didn't think I was a stalker. We both were amazed our paths had never crossed until today.

As she was standing in the doorway, Fran shared one more thing with me. She hoped Dallis was looking down from heaven and could hear our conversation and all the wonderful things that were being said about him. She knew he was wonderful, but there were days, she said, when he would come home from work and feel his life had no purpose or meaning.

"I'm sure he hears us," I told her. He had changed my heart just by two brief encounters in a Christmas aisle. A group of church ladies had also been blessed and enlightened by these two encounters when I passed them on. It was because of Dallis and his hats of honor that I became a mentor to our local students. Every week I played Jinja, Uno, and Hangman with them, and of course supervised homework, trying to help them as they help me. The students and I have learned trust and self-worth, and in doing so we have become forever friends.

Months passed. Many times I visited our local Walmart. One of those times, I was walking down the main aisle, and there to my surprise was Fran Easterday. She was wearing a blue shirt like her husband had worn the day I met him in the Christmas aisle. She was busy at the Walmart register, scanning boxes, bobbles, and groceries with the same busy, service-oriented attitude that I had seen in her husband.

A peaceful, warm feeling came over me as I thought about what an adventure we all had journeyed through. We had started out as strangers in the midst of a Christmas season, doing the normal everyday doings that people do. I thought of all the people who had been touched by a small green box of fifty-count white lights and the shine of a fireman-clerk in the Christmas aisle. Our darkened world had been enlightened because of his example.

Often the ones who are doing the most are deceived in the way they think they are doing nothing. They think they have no purpose, but through their smiles of compassion and their desire to serve others, they touch a lost world, one person at a time. I know this to be true because I was one who was touched.

Happiness is caused by things that happen around you. Circumstances will mar it. But joy flows right on through trouble; joy flows on through the dark; joy flows in the night as well as in the day; joy flows all through persecution and opposition. It is an unceasing fountain bubbling up in the heart, a secret spring the world cannot give or one cannot buy. The Lord gives his people perpetual joy when they walk in obedience to him. Another name for joy is *shine*.

A holy life will produce the deepest impression.

Lighthouses blow no horns; they only shine.

D. L. Moody
American Evangelist, Publisher, Founder
of Moody Bible Institute

-20-

A Real Live Boy

Stories, parables, and fables can play a part in life choices and the molding of character. Could it be that instead of being grumpy, you have chosen to whistle while you work? A love for animals might have started with 101 spotted puppies. Instead of becoming bored or lonely, a bunch of merry mice might have taught you how to make something out of a lot of little nothings. Boys are encouraged to fight the evil villains and slay dragons. Girls sing and hope for the charming prince who will make their lives happy ever after. It's inevitable that who we spend time with will influence us. Who we are among is who we will be like, for good and for bad.

Throughout my childhood and into parenthood, and now as a grandmother, I must say it is the story of the wooden boy that so often still pulls the strings to my heart.

> *Little woodenhead, go play your part,*
> *Bring a little joy to every heart*
> *In a weary world you do your share,*
> *Spreading laughter everywhere*
> —The clock maker's song in *Pinocchio*

129

The simplicity of a children's song can echo a profound message. We all have a part in making merriment for hearts. Our world has become weary of doing good; instead, it seems a duty to be critical. There is surely not laughter everywhere, maybe anywhere.

A merry heart doeth good like a medicine.
(Prov. 17:22)

Raising children can bring joy when they obey rules and follow a parent in example. There comes a time when the strings of guidance and protection are replaced with independence. It is here every parent becomes concerned, knowing one bad choice can ruin a life. Parenting is said to be the most important job and the hardest.

Tell me and I forget, teach me and I may
remember, involve me and I learn.
—Benjamin Franklin

The first day of school is always bittersweet. Wisdom and knowledge are necessary, but trusting the unknown is difficult. Without a parent's guiding strings, the child's choices may not be wise. Will they remember? Will they obey all they have been taught? A little independence mixed with too much confidence can make a child believe he or she knows it all. Where will they go, what might they say, and who will their friends be? These are the heartbeats of a parent. Wanting the best for a child is not about material goods or pleasure. It is about wanting the best character—knowing what is right and doing it.

The love, respect and confidence of my children was the sweetest reward I could receive for my efforts to be the woman I would have them copy.

—Louisa May Alcott

I will instruct thee and teach thee in the way which thou shalt go: I will guide thee with thine eye. (Ps. 32: 8)

Children are a heritage unto the Lord and gifted in their own special ways. They are to be taught to tell the truth and never lie, to be faithful and not deceitful. They should learn to give and not be greedy or steal. They should know kindness and shung conceit. They should be humble and not proud, becoming wise and not foolish. These are the desires of a parent and the guidance to becoming a real live boy.

If you love me, you will keep my commandments. (John 14:14)

Filthy varmints of deception lure young minds with false promises, introducing them to rebellion. Many lessons have they of their own, the opposite of obedience. Letting a conscience have the final authority can prove unwise. Even an adult's conscience can fail and often not even show up. A bad song, a promiscuous place, or the encouragement of an untrue friend can lead anyone into temptation.

Be not deceived; evil communications corrupt good manners. (1 Cor. 15:33)

"I want to be a good boy, but I want to do what I want to do": these are the words of a wooden head. Tests prove the character from within; all it takes is a little time.

> *A man must be a good son, husband and*
> *father, a woman must be a good daughter,*
> *wife and mother, first and foremost.*
> —Teddy Roosevelt

False compassion can be learned at an early age when a child gets all he or she wants. Habitual disobedience means living on a slippery slope and in time will bring ruin. Grabbing for all the heart desires is misleading. Too many holidays and too much pleasure build a whiny, self-willed spirit. Working and enjoying it keep one from becoming slothful, sickly, and deadly. Pleasure has become a crowded park while the workplace has many vacancies. Some pleasures have no rules. Parents are not invited and the clocks have no hands. With no rules and no parents and no time frame, what will become of the children?

A smokescreen of "everyone is doing it" can make wrong look right. It is better to warn again and again that there is a point of no return. There is a fear to be feared. The good boy will yell and run from wrongdoing and the wrong way. A good conscience will scream "Stop!" to bad thoughts and bad reason. It is best to "do right til the stars fall" (Bob Jones, pastor).

Bad can keep a child longer than he or she wants to stay. Bad habits love the keeping on of keeping on. Making bad choices and having bad friends make dreams diminish, homes break, and unconditional love go ignored. Bad makes one disobey one rule and then another, say one unkind word and then another, hurt one heart and then another, tell one lie and then another, look past one truth and then another.

> *He that walketh with wise men shall be wise: but a companion of fools shall be destroyed. (Prov. 13:20)*
>
> *Be sure your sin will find you out. (Num. 32:23)*

There is a sorrow unfamiliar to many, a sorrow that is not ashamed and willing to change for good. Wisdom knows there is a payday someday for unrepented wrongdoing. A conscience is not always trustworthy. It can oversleep or fall behind in its reasoning. Wisdom does not withhold truth nor sincerity. Wisdom has a peace that passes understanding. It is accompanied with gentleness and knowledge. This is a godly sorrow our world does not know and sadly does not want. It is the parent's duty to have and to teach wisdom to the child. It is a child's duty to believe and to trust and to obey.

> *But the wisdom that is from above is first pure, then peaceable, gentle, and easy to be intreated, full of mercy and good fruits, without partiality, and without hypocrisy. (James 3:17)*
>
> *"If we say that we have no sin, we deceive ourselves, and the truth is not in us." (1 John 1:8 kjv.) If we turn over a new leaf and*

> *depend upon conscience and self-will, it will last for only moments. If we choose not wisdom and ignore the facts in our way, there is no reason for the sorrow called godly. We will not prosper in being a real, live boy."*

> *He that covereth his sins shall not prosper: but whoso confesseth and forsaketh shall have mercy. (Prov. 28:13)*

To *repent* is to have a sincere regret or remorse, guilt or shame. It is to change one's mind and want to do right.

> *Lawless are they, that make their will their law.*
> —William Shakespeare

In fables, dreams do come true, In life, a dream come true is a blessing or a miracle. Godly fear and repentance are the powers that keep one's slate clean. Even though you have infirmities, aim for honesty and hold on to integrity. Rejection of truth and habitual sin have big price tags no one can afford. Happy is the man that fears always and hates evil, pride, arrogance, and a forward mouth. Instead, love instruction and bow down to the ears of the wise. There is a way that seems right but leads to death. The fear of the Lord is the beginning of wisdom. (See Prov. 8:10; 9:10; 12:1; 14:12; 22:17; 28:14.)

Son, be careful. Run from sin and be brave. Grab on to righteousness and never let go. Shun selfishness and give unto others, until it hurts. Never, never forget: "Do right til the stars fall."

> *If I must choose between peace and righteousness, I choose righteousness.*
> —Teddy Roosevelt

My Son

My son hear the instruction of thy father, and
    forsake not the instruction of thy mother
    For they shall be an ornament of grace unto
    thy head
My son if sinners entice thee consent thou not
My son walk not thou in the way with them;
    refrain thy foot from their path
For their feet run to evil
So are the ways of every one that is greedy of
    gain
My son if thou wilt receive my words, and hide
    my commandments with thee;
So that thou incline thine ear unto wisdom and
    apply thine heart to understanding;
My son attend unto my wisdom, and bow thine
    ear to my understanding
My son, despise not the chastening of the Lord;
    neither be weary of his correction
My son, attend to my words; incline thine
ear unto my sayings

> Let them not depart from thine eyes; keep them
> in the midst of thine heart
> For they are life unto those that find them, and
> health to all their flesh
> If thou seekest her as silver, and searchest for
> her as for hid treasures;
> Then shalt thou understand the fear of the Lord,
> and find the knowledge of God.
> For length of days, and long life, and peace shall
> they add to thee.
> Let not mercy and truth forsake thee: bind them
> about thy neck; write them upon the table of
> thine heart:
> A wise son maketh a glad father: But a foolish
> son is the heaviness of his mother.

These are the words of King Solomon in the book of Proverbs. He is known to have been the wisest of all men and the son of King David, in the lineage of Jesus Christ. (Pr. 1;8,9,10,15,16,19, 2:1,2 5;1 3;11, 4:20,21,22, 2:4,5, 3:2,3, 10:1)

The wiles of the devil is upon the parent that wants it to be well with their child's soul. It is a must for the parent to be a brave heart and to know the enemy. The choice between right and wrong is a moment-by-moment commission and compromise is lethal. Children do come with an instruction manual; it is the obedience to the ways of the Lord. Dreams can come true if they are approved from on High.

So when wishing upon a star, "I wish above all things that thou mayest prosper" (Deut. 29:9).

It doesn't matter who you are; "God is no respecter of persons" (Rom. 2:11).

Request your heart's desire, "for with God nothing shall be impossible" (Luke 1:3).

It can come true. "Call unto me, and I will answer thee, and shew thee great and mighty things, which thou knowest not" (Jer. 33:3).

It has all to do with your heart. "Create in me a clean heart, O God" (Ps. 51:10).

No requests are too extreme; "ask and it shall be given you" (Matt. 7:7).

And when you wish beyond the stars, "we wish even your perfection" (1 Cor. 13:9).

Praying dreams do come true.

A Real Live Boy

Watch ye therefore, and pray always, that ye may be accounted worthy to escape all these things that shall come to pass, and to stand before the Son of man. (Luke 21:36)

Even a child is known by his doings, whether his work be pure, and whether it be right. (Prov. 20:11)

Deep down in my heart I knew I was doing things not right and mother was continually pleading with me to quit my way of doing and change my way of life and be a better boy. When I quit, I quit all. I'm very glad I did. I'm a good deal like Paul, the things I once loved, I now hate. And then I was saved.
—Sergeant Alvin C. York,
the most decorated American hero
in World War I

I rejoiced greatly that I found of thy children walking in truth. (2 John 1:4)

I ask of myself, "Live a good Christian life."
—Walt Disney

-21-

Warning from Spirits

I can't go to sleep grandma, Conner Jack whispered, as I was tucking him under the covers. Why are you afraid? I asked. I see things moving outside the window and mom says it's just the trees, he replied. That's right Conner, it is, just the trees, what makes you afraid, what do you think it is, if it is not the trees? I ask. I think it is a ghost, do you believe in ghost's grandma? I smiled at my four-year-old grandson and I had to tell him yes, I do believe in ghosts, my dearest and closest forever friend is a Ghost.

Mr. Scrooge

There's Bob Cratchit, my clerk, sitting across the room, laboring as he has for many years, keeping my books of business in order. The glowing lamps help our eyes to stay sharp, while the crackling fire warms us, keeping our fingers limber so we can write comfortably. It is not uncommon for my shop door to fly open and my nephew Fred to appear, his cheery voice bidding us a good day. Before leaving, he insists I come for supper. Often, gazing through the leaded windows onto the streets of London, I thank God for all the blessings he has bestowed upon me.

[As you may already know, Mr. Scrooge was not always a compassionate and grateful man. In fact, he was the complete opposite. But there was one night that brought revelation, repentance, and revival to a dreadful, hopeless, wretched man named Ebenezer Scrooge. This is his story.]

My business partner, Jacob Marley, and I had fared well. We were distinguished men who had earned a seat on the London Exchange and were admired in our money lending. We cared little of what went on outside our counting house; the making of money was our business and, to us, all that truly mattered. Even though Marley's death took me by surprise, business went on as usual. There is always money to be earned.

One night, everything would change: the seventh anniversary of my partner's death. I distinctly remember it was a very dark and frigid night. I could see my breath while walking home. As I unlatched my door, I thought only of the warm bowl of gruel near the fire and then of retiring within the curtains of my bed. As I sat near the crackling flames, sipping my broth, I listened to the music of the whistling night air hitting the branches against the window.

Suddenly the old, cobwebbed bell on the wall began to ring. I was startled to hear it and amazed that it still worked. Many years had passed since I heard this bell chime, too many to count. Someone must have miscalculated and was visiting the wrong address, I thought. In time they would be on their way and leave me to my solace.

Again I was disturbed, now by a clanking noise coming from outside my chamber door. Louder the strange noise became as it drew nearer. Frightened as I was, I couldn't believe my eyes when a shadow of a man walked directly through my multiply locked door. I set my gruel down. My lips trembled as I spoke. "Who are you and what do you want?"

Surprisingly, he answered me directly. "I want much" were his words. He went on to explain that in life he had been my business partner and friend, Jacob Marley. I wondered if maybe my gruel had been spoiled and I was having a reaction. Perhaps he was a hallucination of some sort?

He, becoming angry, fiercely shook the chains and money boxes that were wrapped about his transparent soul. Horror grabbed my attention. When he asked if I believed in him and his words, I said, "I do, I do!"

He went on more calmly to say he would never know peace or a feeling of rest. There was in all eternity not enough regret to amend the opportunities he had missed. "It is too late," he said sadly. I tried to interrupt, to encourage him about the fact of what a fine businessman he had been, but instead he became even angrier. "Mankind was my business and the common welfare was too," he expounded. "Charity, mercy, forbearance, and benevolence were all my business. The dealings of my trade were but a drop of water in the vast ocean compared to what it all should have been." He then reminded me that in all his life, he never walked beyond our counting house, what now he called "a money-changing hole."

I became ill with his words. I highly disagreed with his reasoning and attitude. This was not the Jacob Marley I had known. Why was he so provoked at the life we both worked so long and hard to achieve? Why had it brought him to such a place of despair? I didn't understand why he was being so hard on himself and bringing me all this pain and agony. "Bring me some comfort instead of all this gloom and doom," I asked him.

Sadly, the spirit told me he had none to give. He moved toward an open window, and I could see his time with me was short. "I came to warn you," he said. My path in life was familiar to him, and my journey had the same promised ending. He told me I would receive the visitation of three spirits. He believed that without those visits, I would continue on as he had and shun all hope. For me too there would be no escape from a horrid future. "Look to see me no more."

As he stepped to the open window, his exhausted breath penetrated my bedchambers one more time. "For your own sake, remember what has passed between us."

The spirit of Marley fell into the smoke-thickened stench of a dreadful realm. I could hear sounds of wailing and lamentations of regret. Quickly latching the window, I crawled beneath my covers. As I laid my head on my pillow, I knew it was rest I needed. I drifted into a deep sleep.

A bright light prompted me to awake. I covered my head, but it had no effect in shutting out the brilliance. Opening my eyes, I saw something or somebody standing very near. Quiet, it was quiet. "Are you the spirit my friend Marley foretold would come and visit me?"

"Yes," it said. It told me it was there to guide me in and through my past. I could see a very tall cap under this spirit's arm. I thought it might be a good idea if it were to bonnet the rays that seemed to be coming from its head and were quite discomforting to my eyes. Had it done so, the way of truth and lessons from my past would be darkened. I would not be able to see nor learn, it explained. I knew this spirit was there for the same purpose as Marley: the good of my soul.

This unearthly being somehow—I can't explain how—took me on a journey into my past. We visited places where I had played as a child. Old friends were so close I could touch them. Though I tried to call out, they could not see nor hear me. It was good to remember and laugh, but the past has its heartaches. I could see my father, and I was reminded of the disappointment he carried through life. My mother had died young from childbirth—mine.

My father was always distant to me. I believed he blamed me for the loss of his dear wife. Did this hurt my heart as a child? Did it affect the molding of my character as a man? Was I less than I could have been? It was as if those beaming rays put my heart on trial. As I struggled for answers, I was whisked away into another time in my past.

It was closing time, and everyone was in a rush. There I was, a young apprentice. Mr. Fizziwig, my boss, and a fine boss indeed, was preparing for a party. Music played and many fancy foods complemented the tables. It was not uncommon for such a man as Mr. Fizziwig to celebrate with his friends and employees; that's just who he was. Belle was there, beautiful Belle. We danced and shared our dreams. We were to marry, but I thought it best we wait until my finances were more sizable and secure. As years passed, Belle wearied in her waiting and untied me from any commitment. Seeing her, I wondered if I had made a dreadful mistake. Again I was led away.

Voices echoed across a snow-covered street where I now stood. I could hear Belle's voice laughing and talking with what I believed to be her family, a fine-looking family indeed. I thought for a moment that this family could have been mine.

The children had been given a gift by their father; it was plain to see he had come from town and brought them something. The tall gentleman was telling Belle he had seen an old friend of hers and wanted her to guess who it might be. Belle became frustrated in the silly game and blurted out a quick answer. It was my name: Ebenezer Scrooge! I was shocked and looked to the spirit for a response. There was none. Belle's husband said yes, and went on to describe me as a sad and lonely soul, sitting in the window of my business with only a single candle to work by. As if that weren't enough, after hesitating, Belle referred to me as a poor, wretched man.

I wanted to see and hear no more. I demanded the spirit take me from this place. I grabbed the pointed bonnet from under the spirit's arm, and with great strength I forced it onto its head. To see and hear no more was my greatest desire. Instantly I was within the walls of my bedchamber. I wanted nothing more than sleep.

I was awakened again by a call of "Ebenezer Scrooge! Ebenezer Scrooge!" Was I dreaming? Through the crack of one eye, I could see a festive collection of holly, mistletoe, and ivy hanging off the mirrors on my walls. Opening another eye, I saw lit candles and a blaze in the chimney. Turkeys, geese, pigs, mince pies, plum puddings, apples, oranges, and big glass bowls of punch nestled in every corner of the room.

My eyes were now wide open. Among all this grandeur sat a handsomely dressed spirit. I could plainly see he was part of this magnificent season that proclaimed peace on earth and goodwill toward men, a yearly celebration I had chosen for many years to ignore. Following the festive spirit's soft commands, I touched his emerald robe and was lifted into the brisk but calm night.

I passed the stars that shone brightly, and looked down upon my city. Glistening bells rang on the horses, and laughter came from every cobblestone street. Candied fruits were stacked in the store windows, while homes displayed decorations that echoed joy to the world. A church door opened, and I could see the pews were packed. "Silent Night" and the birth of a newborn King were being sung.

The spirit was busy dropping blessed dust onto a house. It was the home of my clerk, Bob Cratchit. In the blink of an eye, there we stood in the midst of a prayer. Then Bob and his family began to eat. My thoughts were with the bird on the table; I had never seen one so small.

I noticed a crutch near the smallest member of the family, a little boy they called Tiny Tim. The spirit gave me a look. I didn't know why; maybe because I didn't bow my head in prayer? Everyone lifted their glasses as Bob proposed a toast to the founder of their feast—his employer, Ebenezer Scrooge. I kind of puffed up at the sight of the glasses in the air. Then, one by one, each glass was lowered to the cotton tablecloth. The mother refused to toast a stingy, odious, mean, hard, unfeeling old man. She went on to say it was his tightness that brought hurt to their family. If that weren't bad enough, all the children agreed!

Thank goodness for a wise father, who soothed them all to repent of such remarks. I wondered how their food could be digested properly with such horrid attitudes. The spirit, with another one of those looks, motioned me away.

My feet now stood on the crowded London streets full of frolic. The spirit led me onto a porch with a beautiful lacquered door.

It was my nephew Fred's home. We entered without a knock. We could hear him explaining to a handsome crowd the reason for my absence. I was his only living relative, and it was plain to see he was sorry I couldn't be there. He made it clear I thought a bountiful dinner was a waste of one's earnings, and this seasonal celebration was nothing but a "bah, humbug."

Fred's motives were pure. I knew he was much like his mother, my dear sister, bless her heart. She's been gone a long time. I was all Fred had, and he was right about how I felt regarding this money-wasting season.

I could see his guests possessed neither respect nor admiration for his uncle. Instead I was made fun of in the playing of a word game. When filling in the answer to "What is tighter than a _ _ _ _?" for which the intended answer was *drum*, Fred's wife responded, "Tighter than your uncle's purse strings." Fred told her that my offences carried their own punishment, and that she should speak well of me. I got no humor from their laughter, seeing it was at my expense. I was again ready to leave this place of revelation.

Before I could request departure, I found myself in a dark alley with a stench quite unbearable. Fires were burning in rusted barrels. Everyone around me was dressed in rags, crying for food, and complaining they had no work. "Bad times have come to many. Even if they do work, the infested, diseased workhouses bring an early death," said the spirit, looking to me for a response.

The putrid smell and morbid scene were more than I could bear. The merriment of the season surely was not in this place. Being very uncomfortable, I suggested in a pleasant manner that it might be best if we both returned home. Turning back to the spirit, I saw only thick fog. "Where are you?" I asked. None of the spirits had ever left me alone. In waiting, I became uneasy. The spirit was nowhere to be seen. I called louder into the outer darkness, "Come back, spirit. I want to talk. Maybe

I have been wrong on some things. Have pity on me this time. Please, spirit, don't leave me alone. What have I done that I should be abandoned?"

The frozen wind through the barren trees was the only voice that answered. Sitting in the dampness of this black night, for the first time I trembled with a haunting fear of being forever alone.

A shadow approached. I hoped it would be the merry spirit returning. Instead, the silhouette of what seemed a solemn phantom came closer and closer. The image was like a vapor, draped and hooded so as to have form. Protruding from under his cloak came a long finger pointing. His presence brought no rays of light and no merriment of any sort, only an eerie silence.

Of all the spirits I knew, this one was to be feared the most. Shivering, I asked, "Am I in the presence of the spirit of Christmas yet to come, to see the things that have not yet happened?"

There was no answer.

I prepared myself to bear his lack of communication and dreadful company. "Lead on, spirit," I told him. With a great crack and a flash from the black sky, there appeared a pillared hall of exchange, a place I knew well. Many businessmen, fine and proper, were discussing money and their trade. I was not eavesdropping, but three men stood near, discussing another matter: a scratch of a man who had gotten his own at last.

"Where did he leave his money?" one asked.

"Probably to his company. I don't know," said another.

I could hear plainly as the men spoke of a small funeral. They had no interest in attending—that is, unless there was a meal provided. They laughed profusely as their meeting broke up; their watches spoke to them that trade was waiting. Looking closely at their faces, I realized I had personally done business with these men. Speaking abruptly, I asked the spirit if these men had no respect for the dead. The spirit stood cold, as if I was of no importance to him. With another clap of thunder, we stood by the bed of a dead man.

I could see the outline of a body as it lay covered by a sheet from head to toe. I wanted to pull the cover off to see who lay beneath. Could this be the same man who was referred to as "a scratch" by the businessmen? Why did he lie there alone? Was there no one to feel grief for this lonely dead person? Did he not have family or friends? Why did I have to be brought to such a morbid place as this?

The spirit led me away. We stood in a dimly lighted entranceway. I could see it was an ungodly, terrible place I had been taken to. Dealings were going on. I hesitated to enter because of the atrocious odor, but at the same time, the circle of thieves intrigued me. "How much will you give?" one of them asked. Another unfolded a soiled cloth with a gold pocket watch and a chain inside. Holding it to his ear, the filthy man listened to the chimes. Curtains, bed curtains, and even the rings that held them were another purchase. I could see they were possessions of the dead man. The robbers had stolen them for gain.

"He was a wicked old screw and had no one to take care of him after he was gone," an old lady said. The circle of dingy grave robbers squawked in laughter at their morbid jokes.

Moving closer to look at the treasures they were bartering over, I thought they looked very similar to my belongings. "Blow the whistle on these thieves," I thought, but then no. These couldn't be my belongings. I was still alive. Instead I became furious and outspoken once again at their lack of emotion for the dead man.

There was never time for rage. The spirit led me on. I wondered what the spirit was thinking. We once again stood among Bob Cratchit's family. The children were reading a Bible story by candlelight, a story about suffering children entering into a great kingdom.

Their mother was sewing. I could see her eyes were reddened with tears. She warned the children that they should be happy when their father returned. Somewhat late, he entered and explained he had stopped by the grave of Tiny Tim, the smallest child who had sat at the dinner table with a crutch nearby. "A kind man gave a more than kind condolence in town today and was saddened for our loss," Bob told his wife. He went on to share that it had been my nephew Fred.

Seeing the grief this family bore, I wanted to see no more. I begged once again to be taken to my home. The draped ghost only did as he knew to do and ignored my every word.

Returning to the streets of London, we passed my place of employment. I peeked through the leaded glass to see how I would fare in the future. The furniture looked unfamiliar, as did the workers. The spirit hurried me along. I could feel the crunch of snow beneath my bed slippers. In the dark of night, the only glow was off the white stones lined up in rows around us. We were standing in the midst of a very large graveyard.

While walking with these spirits, I had become familiar with their attributes and learned they all had purpose. I had endured my best friend's death, which had replaced my peace with doom. A haunting light affected my mind, enlightening old thoughts and choices that portrayed me as unwise and selfish. I had never accomplished all that I could have. In the name of merriment and the holiness of season, I had been shown what others thought of my life. My greed and distance had affected the world around me, and not for the betterment of mankind.

Now as I stood in the yard of stones and looked upon this last ghost, I pleaded that his silence be broken. Of all the lessons of the spirits, there was only one I could not bear, and it was the dreadful silence this last haunting spirit bore.

"Answer me one question, spirit," I pleaded. "Are these shadows of things that will be, or are they shadows of things that may be? Let me behold what I shall be in the days to come."

He would not answer me and only pointed to a grave.

Moving closer, I could see an unkempt stone covered with snow. Trembling, I looked back to the spirit and pleaded one more time that he talk to me. "Was I the man on the bed covered by the sheet?" I asked.

The ghost once again pointed to the stone. I knelt and brushed the snow away and read the writing etched into its face. It read, *"Ebenezer Scrooge."* Clutching his draped garment, I cried, "No, spirit, no! Hear me, spirit! I am not the man I was. I will not be the man I must have been. Why show me this if I am past all hope? Pity me, good spirit; assure me that I may yet change these shadows you have shown me by an altered life! I see how my past has hardened my reasoning. I have ignored the true meaning of a merry season. I know I have lived in a way that I cared not for others and feared not for my future. My eyes now can see that you are right and I have been wrong. I will remember the lessons of the past, the teaching of the present, and the understanding of my future. I will try to keep them all the year through. I will never again shut out the truth you have shown me. Oh spirit, please tell me there is a way for me to sponge away the writing on this stone!"

True repentance is to feel pain, sorrow, or regret for something done or spoken that has caused injury to or wounded the feelings of another. A person can repent only what he or she has done or said.

Was my crying plea sincere? Many would be skeptical. Was I truly a repentant man, or was I just afraid of death? Words are cheap. Knowing my character, few had faith in me.

A Doomed Friend

*And some save with fear, pulling them
out of the fire; hating even the garment
spotted by the flesh.*

—Jude 23

*For what shall it profit a man, if he shall
gain the whole world, and lose his own
soul? Or what shall a man give in exchange
for his soul?*

—Mark 8:36–37

Jacob Marley's spirit had traveled from a place of eternal
torment to warn me. Death had taught a lesson that he had
chosen to ignore from life. How he came to my chambers, I do
not know. In fear and trembling he wanted me to believe in his
message. He knew my last hope was in the spirits yet to come.

*Who hath warned you to flee from the
wrath to come? (Luke 3:7)*

The first spirit came as promised and traveled in my past. He
bore an uncomfortable beam that was most irritating. The rays
illuminated the hurts from the back burners of my past, ones
that to me were best forgotten. In his message, I could see hurt.
People do hurt other people, and bad choices live on to condemn
us in heart. The great light was to have purpose, direction,
and correction. Thinking this spirit to be most contentious, I
bonneted the rays and chose to continue as before, satisfying
my own desires.

The second spirit came embracing a present merriment and a felicity of faith. He brought much attention to relationships and helping others. I had worked hard for what I had. My comfort was of my own making, and his ways was foolish and brought much anguish to me. I chose to be reserved so as not to offend, I could see he felt mocked, accusing me of insincerity. What he believed to be gospel, I saw as humbug. I rejected what I thought was again a contentious spirit. He left me alone, all alone. In his uncaring departure, the third spirit appeared.

The third and last spirit finally appeared, bearing my future—a time I thought would take care of itself. I could see this spirit was different from the others and greatly to be feared. There was a distance between him and me, and no communication. I begged him on several occasions to reply to my inquiries; he never once answered my call. I was on my own as I watched this judging ghost. For some odd reason I couldn't get Marley's voice out of my mind. The beaming rays of past truth and present time were echoing my acts. I thought to be good, and now my own heart was condemning me. I knew that if I chose to laugh, walk away, and ignore them all, the last spirit would usher me into an eternal state of doom.

"I am not the man I was. I will not be the man I must have been. Assure me that I may yet change. Oh, spirit, please tell me there is a way!" I cried.

Marley's predictions held true. Our lives together gradually became corrupt through the love of money. We lost affection and communication in our lives and with others. Even if I wanted to be a better man, I knew that wasn't enough. A spiritual awakening is what I needed, and that is why the spirits came. I needed a saving grace; I needed a pardon from all my wretchedness. Acknowledging this, I decided to trust in another.

> *I am the way, the truth, and the life. (John 14:6)*

> *Whosoever shall call upon the name of the Lord shall be saved. (Rom. 10:13)*

> *Therefore if any man be in Christ, he is a new creature: old things are passed away; behold all things are become new. (2 Cor. 5:17)*

Awakening from my sleep, I found myself on the floor of my bedchamber, praying and begging forgiveness for the contemptible life I had lived and the ungodly man I had let myself become. The men and women in the streets were right when speaking of my reputation. I was a tight-fisted, nose to the grindstone, covetous, wretched old sinner of a man. Many thought my heart had no warmth and my eyes seemed evil. It was true I never wanted merriment. Distance was all I cared to have from my fellow man. My life consisted only of making money, and I ignored even my own family.

I confessed openly to the deeply afflicted, distressed, miserable old man that I was. I hid nothing because I wanted to be forgiven and saved from a life of woe. I wanted to be different. I wanted to care. I wanted mankind to be my friends. I wanted to treat everyone equally and learn to always forgive, whatever the cost. I wanted to love. I want to *believe*.

> *Amazing grace how sweet the sound! That*
> *saved a wretch like me!*
> *I once was lost but now am found; Was*
> *blind, and now I see.*
> *How precious did that grace appear, The*
> *hour I first Believed?*
> —John Newton

A Changed Man

These are the testimonies of the people in my city of London, where I have lived my entire life. They know me for who I was and who I have become. What do people say?

"He has become a wonderful uncle and keeps a great relationship with his sister's family."

"He attends church when the doors are open, and others' needs are his deeds."

"The children's welfare has become a great interest to him, and the poor have become his business."

"Dressed in his best, he tips his hat and greets everyone daily in the streets of old England with a cheery good morning and a blessed good night."

"As for his clerk, Bob Cratchit, and his family, they are all well. Mr. Cratchit received a raise, and his son Tiny Tim has received medical care. Now the boy's health has been restored completely."

"Mr. Scrooge is now a second father to Tiny Tim and a good friend to everyone—the best man the old city has ever known."

Many laughed to see such a change in an old screw; and let them. Nothing ever happens on this globe for good, at which some only laugh. I have learned that. As they are, I once was. They just don't understand. I will never forget the teachings that were passed before me by the spirits. They are now principles that I live by, principles that come from within, where a heart has been born again. I, Ebenezer Scrooge, am now one who can keep merriment all the year through.

Therefore we ought to give the more earnest heed to the things, which we have

heard, lest at any time we should let them slip. For if the word spoken by angels was stedfast, and every transgression and disobedience received a just recompense of reward. How shall we escape, if we neglect so great salvation? (Heb. 2:1-4)

God bless us, every one.

I don't think I will ever tire of this most blessed story. The original version was written by Charles Dickens. Ebenezer Scrooge was a wretched man, destined for eternal doom. But he had a friend who could warn him from the depths of his own eternal despair. When the warning failed, that friend reached out one more time and called for the heavenly spirits.

There is a reaching out in our universe to every living soul. Mr. Scrooge, still breathing, had time—time to see the past, the present, and his future. He read the spirits carefully and changed his mind. He trusted in another way to secure his eternal soul, and *believed.*

I am come that they might have life, and that they might have it more abundantly.
—John 10:10

We love him, because he first loved us.
—1 John 4:19

-22-

Another Story, Another Spirit, Another Ghost

When passing from this world to the next, we will leave our mortal bodies behind. We will pass through the air in spirit form. "We are confident, I say, and willing rather to be absent from the body, and to be present with the Lord" (2 Cor. 5:8).

God's Spirit is invisible. He is a person, he has a personality, and he wants to be known. He wants us to ask and to seek him out. If we knock, he will open the door to all understanding. In Spirit form, God is known as the Holy Ghost or the Holy Spirit. Jesus refers to him as a personal Comforter who lives within the hearts of all believers since Jesus ascended to his Father. This Spirit of God is first mentioned in Genesis 1:2: "And the earth was without form, and void; and darkness was upon the face of the deep. And the Spirit of God moved upon the face of the waters. And God said, let there be light: and there was light."

There are other references to the Holy Spirit in the Old Testament:

> *And Moses said unto the people, Fear ye not, stand still, and see the salvation of*

the Lord. The Lord shall fight for you, and ye shall hold your peace. And the Lord said unto Moses, Wherefore criest thou unto me? Speak unto the children of Israel that they go forward. But lift up thou thy rod, and stretch out thy hand over the sea, and divide it: and the children of Israel shall go on dry ground through the midst of the sea. It was then by God Almighty's command and his Spirit's power a nation was saved. The Egyptians shall know that I am the Lord. (Exod. 14:13-31)

The wicked king of Syria warred against Israel as he came down to spy in Dothan on Elisha and his men. He sent thither horses and chariots and a great host: and they came by night, and compassed the city about. And when the man of God was risen early, behold an host compassed the city both with horses and chariots. And his servant said unto him, "Alas my master! How shall we do?" It was than the great prophet Elisha prayed for the power of the almighty God in heaven. And Elisha prayed, and said, "Lord, I pray thee, open his eyes, that he may see." By the power of his Spirit; the Lord opened the eyes of the young man; and he saw: and behold the mountain was full of horses and chariots of fire round about Elisha. (2 Kings 6:8-23)

The hand of the Lord was upon me, and carried me out in the spirit of the Lord, and set me down in the midst of the valley, which was full of bones. And caused me to pass by them round about: and behold, there were very many in the open valley; and lo they were very dry. And he said unto me, Son of man, can these bones live? And I answered O Lord God, thou knowest. Again he said unto me, Prophesy upon these bones, and say unto them, o ye dry bones, hear the word of the Lord. Thus saith the Lord God unto these bones; Behold, I will cause breath to enter into you, and ye shall live: I will bring flesh upon you, and cover you with skin, and put breath in you, and ye shall live; and ye shall know I am the Lord. So I prophesied as he commanded me, and the breath came into them, and they lived, and stood up upon their feet, an exceeding great army. Yes they shall know when I take you out of your graves and put into your chest a new heart, no longer stony and a new spirit, mine. You will walk in my statutes and keep my judgments and I will save you from your uncleanness. By his Great Spirit it is to leave an everlasting impression; and ye shall know that I am the Lord thy God. (Ezek. 37:1-14)

And of course there are many references to the Holy Spirit in the New Testament:

> *Now the birth of Jesus Christ was on this wise: when as his mother Mary was espoused to Joseph, before they came together, she was found with child of the Holy Ghost. For he shall save his people from their sins. (Matt. 1:18-21)*

> *And, behold there was a man in Jerusalem, whose name was Simeon; and the same man was just and devout, waiting for the consolation of Israel: and the Holy Ghost was upon him. And it was revealed unto him by the Holy Ghost, that he should not see death, before he had seen the Lord's Christ. And he came by the Spirit into the temple: and when the parents brought in the child Jesus, to do for him after the custom of the law, Then took he him up in his arms and blessed God and said, Lord, now lettest thou thy servant depart in peace, according to thy word: For mine eyes have seen thy salvation, which thou hast prepared before the face of all people. A light to lighten the Gentiles, and the glory of thy people Israel. (Luke 2:25-32)*

And I will pray the Father, and he shall give you another Comforter, that he may abide with you forever. (John 14:16)

Nevertheless, I tell you the truth; It is expedient for you that I go away: for if I go not away, the Comforter will not come unto you; but if I depart, I will send him unto you. (John 16:7)

But when the Comforter is come, whom I will send unto you from the Father, even the Spirit of truth, which proceeded from the Father, he shall testify of me. (John 15:26)

But the Comforter, which is the Holy Ghost, whom the Father will send in my name, he shall teach you all things, and bring all things to your remembrance, whatsoever I have said unto you. (John 14:26)

Yet a little while, and the world seeth me no more; but ye see me: because I live, ye shall live also. (John 14:19)

O boundless love divine, how shall this tongue of mine
To wondering mortals tell, the matchless grace divine

> *That I a child of hell should in his image*
> *shine*
> *The Comforter has come*
> > —William J. Kirkpatrick,
> > "The Comforter Has Come"

> He lives, he lives, Christ Jesus lives today!
> He walks with me and talks with me, along life's
> narrow way.
> He lives, he lives, salvation to impart!
> You ask me how I now he lives? He lives within
> my heart.
> > —Alfred H. Ackley, "He Lives"

The story of Mr. Scrooge has echoed down through the years. We as humans still wonder about spirits, about what is true and what is not true. Three people could open an old King James Bible and begin to read for answers to such questions. As one turns the pages, many of the words may seem hard to understand or difficult to pronounce. The stories may seem boring. When ended, the lesson is missed and time wasted.

Another may read the same pages and discover many blessings and promises. The words they hold precious and trust to be true. With this trust, the second reader grows to believe and profess the name of Christian.

There is a third reader who often stands alone. He is drawn to the Word of God and finds it hard to put the Book down. The passages speak to him in a way that becomes real. It is, to him, the breath of God. His ways become serious because of who is leading him. Fearfulness and sorrow in wrongdoing are his attributes.

Why the difference, you ask? It is the influence of a person. It is the teaching and the leading of the Holy Spirit of God.

> *No man can come to me, except the Father*
> *which hath sent me draw him: and I will*
> *raise him up at the last day.*
>
> —John 6:44

-23-

Meet the Holy Spirit, the Comforter

The Holy Spirit is *omnipresent*, present in all places at the same time, ubiquitous, existing everywhere.

> *Whither shall I go from thy Spirit? Or whither shall I flee from thy presence? If I ascend up into heaven, thou art there: If I make my bed in hell, behold, thou art there. If I take the wings of the morning, and dwell in the uttermost parts of the sea; even there shall thy hand lead me, and thy right hand shall hold me. (Ps. 139:7-10)*

He is *omniscient*, possessing complete, unlimited knowledge. He knows all things at once; his knowledge is unbounded or infinite.

> *Doest thou know the balancing of the clouds, the wondrous works of him that is perfect in knowledge. (Job 37:16)*

Such knowledge is too wonderful for me, it is high, I cannot attain unto it. (Ps. 139:6)

He is *omnipotent*, all-powerful, and in so being, created our world and everything in and about it. This word in strictness can be applied only to God. He has the attribute of supreme power. He is unstoppable and has unlimited ability in every work.

And I heard as it were the voice of a great multitude, and as the voice of many waters, and as the voice of mighty thunderings, saying Alleluia: for the Lord God omnipotent reigneth. (Rev. 19:6)

All power is given unto me in heaven and in earth. Go ye therefore, and teach all nations, baptizing them in the name of the Father, and of the Son, and of the Holy Ghost: Teaching them to observe all things whatsoever I have commanded you: and lo, I am with you alway, even until the end of the world. (Matt. 28:18-20)

Now the God of hope fill you with all joy and peace in believing, that ye may abound in hope, through the power of the Holy Ghost. (Rom. 15:13)

It is the Spirit that quickeneth; the flesh profiteth nothing: the words I speak unto

> *you, they are spirit, and they are life.*
> *(John 6:63)*

Quickeneth means to stimulate, increase, bring to life. It is an understanding made real, a keener perception, reviving, convicting, cheering, reinvigorating, and refreshing.

The Holy Spirit is likened unto a rich, well-watered tree of life, healthy and blooming with spiritual fruits of understanding, all truth, and a drawing power that wants to do right. Love, joy, peace, gentleness, goodness, faith, meekness, temperance, and long-suffering will change one to be something other than what one was. All of the fruits are vital. Even though it is hard to swallow and may seem bitter, long-suffering is a fruit of the Spirit that can glorify God or change a heart as no other fruit can. It is no wonder Mr. Scrooge could say, after becoming sincerely sorry for all his wrongdoings and sincerely receiving forgiveness from on high, that he was not the man he once was. The Holy Spirit had entered his heart, and there followed much fruit.

Sin will take us farther than we want to go, keep us longer than we want to stay and cost us more than we want to pay. It did Jacob Marley, and it did Mr. Scrooge. They both testified this to be true. They both ignored the spiritual health of their souls. It was too late for Jacob Marley. Though Mr. Scrooge had lost many blessings of life, he was miraculously warned in a dream.

Sin is a wrongdoing according to moral and religious standards. According to biblical standards, it is the voluntary departure of a moral agent from a known rule of rectitude or duty prescribed by God. It is any voluntary transgression of his divine law or violation of a divine command. It can be the neglect of a known duty, or it can be an evil thought,

It is said that sin is a wrong that hurts us, while evil sin is a wrong that hurts others. All sin (wrongdoing and wrong thinking) needs to be acknowledged and dealt with immediately, moment by moment. Get rid of sin of any kind.

One Unforgivable Sin

Psychology books say the highest form of abuse is the act of ignoring or rejecting another person: making another feel unwanted, belittled, unintelligent, defeated, humiliated, or embarrassed. It is a form of disrespect. The afflicted one can often become hopeless as this continual treatment becomes unbearable, to the point that their health, physically and mentally, is endangered.

This severe trauma is often associated with situations of power imbalance and can end in a form of corruption. In divorce courts, this treatment is labeled as extreme mental cruelty and is grounds for separation and, often, divorce.

There is only one sin in the Bible that God will never forgive, and it is not murder or the killing of oneself. There are a lot of heinous crimes we can think of. Though God does judge, there is only one sin he will never forgive.

> *But he that shall blaspheme against the*
> *Holy Ghost hath never forgiveness, but is in*
> *danger of eternal damnation. (Mark 3:29)*

Blasphemy, to God, is an injury because it denies him what is due and belongs to him. It attributes to him that which is not agreeable to his nature; it ignores or rejects his divine plan and purpose. Blasphemy against the Holy Ghost is the fact that we ignore his presence and his purpose. By turning our backs and hardening our hearts, we sign an eternal document of doom. It is not his choice; it is ours.

Mr. Scrooge, having been hurt and neglected as a child, might have carried an inward injury of heart into adulthood. Left alone to our own reasoning, we often make bad choices and are poor counsel to ourselves. We think we have made our own way and are safe. God is grieved that we have left him, turned our backs to his way.

Hurt can disease the heart while it blames or ignores his forgiving, saving, and healing power. Hurt can grow into bitterness and then hate. It is like the stages of a cancer. This condition of heart makes us unstable in thought and deed as we try to find happiness within the pride of life. In so doing we neglect salvation and become what we like to call "self-made men." Self leads to separation and doom. We have grieved God's Spirit by ignoring him—the one and only unforgivable sin.

> *If we say that we have no sin, we deceive*
> *ourselves, and the truth is not in us. If we*
> *confess our sins, he is faithful and just to*

> *forgive us our sins, and to cleanse us from all unrighteousness. If we say that we have not sinned, we make him a liar, and his word is not in us. (1 John 1:8-10)*

To *grieve* is to feel pain of heart, to sorrow or mourn, to be afflicted, or to suffer.

A *grievance* is a formal written complaint that alleges a wrongdoing, inequity, or injustice committed by a person against another. God files a grievance against Christians in the book of Ephesians:

> *And grieve not the Holy Spirit of God, whereby ye are sealed unto the day of redemption. Let all bitterness, and wrath, and anger, and clamor, and evil speaking, be put away from you, with all malice. And be ye kind one to another, tenderhearted, forgiving one another even as God for Christ's sake hath forgiven you. (Eph. 4: 30-32)*

"I shall never know the comfort of peace or the feeling of rest."

"I thought it more important to be busy in life with greed, which I called success. I embraced lies that I called wisdom."

"I believed in what I thought was good, but instead brought a horrid and diminishing future."

Jacob Marley wanted his lifelong friend, Ebenezer, to understand the horridness of rejecting truth and ignoring one's spiritual estate. The Spirit of God can be grieved in a way God calls blasphemy, to the point that he walks away, never to return.

> *And the Lord said, My spirit shall not always strive with man. (Gen. 6:3)*
>
> *And in hell he lift up his eyes, being in torments. (Luke 16:23)*
>
> *Almost thou persuadest me to be a Christian. (Acts 26:28)*
>
> *Breathe on me, Breath of God, Fill me with life anew*
> *That I may love what Thou dost love, And do what Thou wouldst do*
>
> *Breathe on me Breath of God, So shall I never die,*
> *But live with Thee the perfect life Of Thine eternity*

—Edwin Hatch, "Breathe on Me, Breath of God"

"Do you believe in ghosts, Grandma?"

"Yes, Conner Jack. My dearest and closest friend is a Ghost. He is the Holy Ghost, God's Spirit. He is my Comforter. He lives within my heart.

"I love you, Conner Jack."

-24-

A Wonderful Life

"God, oh God, dear Father in heaven."

"I'm not a praying man, but if you're up there and you can hear me, show me the way."

"I'm at the end of my rope. Show me the way, God."

In the Christmas classic, *It's a Wonderful Life*, this was the whispered prayer of George Bailey as he sat on a bar stool on Christmas Eve. Anyone could see by his countenance that something was dreadfully wrong. A man who many would say was living the American Dream had come to a state of hopelessness and was contemplating suicide. How could this happen?

In the United States, every 12.5 minutes, someone loses his or her life to suicide. One million people attempt suicide annually, and 1.5 million years of life are stolen every year by suicide (information courtesy of the American Foundation for Suicide Prevention).

The American Dream

What is the American Dream? Being brought up in a small town? That does have its advantages. But dreams are for everyone, anywhere: knowing your neighbor by name, being friendly and kind because you want to be, embracing good moral standards.

Grandparents and parents were taught to live by the Golden Rule and expected the same from their children. "Do unto others as you would like them to do unto you." This was a rule respected by all men and women. Children were raised to respect their elders and be polite, often quiet! These lessons were passed down from generation to generation in the dreams of America. If you didn't work, you didn't eat. When it came to marriage, it wasn't unusual for friends or childhood sweethearts to unite with the encouragement and blessings of their parents.

Old homes are always available and can be purchased for practically nothing. If you are willing to clean up and fix up, in time anyone can have the apple pie, hot dog dream come true. America has known hard times, and there are and will be days and years when jobs get scarce, but with determination, a devotion not to quit, and wisdom or counsel in money management, it is possible to live the American Dream. It's not just about money and comfort. It's respect and dignity to all, good morals, hard work, doing what's right, never forgetting the cost of freedom, and having the ability to achieve while wanting a future over which the same flag of conviction will forever wave.

George Bailey inherited a building and loan company, and in so doing found a way to multiply this dream.

A *humanitarian* is one who has concerns for improving the welfare and happiness of people. Humanitarians possess kind feelings and sympathy toward others, especially when it comes to relieving people in distress—those who are helpless or defenseless. They are opposed to cruelty, not jealous or envious, and often make themselves vulnerable in order to achieve the best for another.

George viewed his life as a less than what he could have been. He had always hoped to leave his small town, a place he thought held little opportunity. His blueprint of dreams was to travel and design high buildings and fast trains. Life can often throw us a curveball that's hard to understand. Many believe that when this happens, it's for a purpose, and the One who throws the ball has a name.

Fate is an ultimate agency by which the order of things is presumably prescribed. It is a predetermined destiny, a prophetic declaration of what must be. If we dig even deeper into the meaning of this agent, it is said to have purpose and often a reason that may be missed. Many believe it has a spiritual side, a divine calling. It is then called providence.

Providence is primarily a decree or word pronounced by God, a fixed sentence by which the order of things is prescribed. Hence it is an inevitable necessity, a destiny that depends on a superior cause and is uncontrollable. It is an event predetermined, a lot in life. It is said to be a source of great consolation to good men for a great purpose, brought about by God's guidance, judgment, and management.

> *"For my thoughts are not your thoughts, neither are your ways my ways," saith the Lord. "For as the heavens are higher than the earth, so are my ways higher than your ways, and my thoughts than your thoughts." (Isa. 55:8-9)*

In a marriage in which the partners complement each other while working hard together and enjoying one another's company, many would say they are on the same page or they were made for each other. Hearing the tone of their voices as they say each other's names, you know their love and respect is deep. Virtues don't come easy, but through good and consistent upbringing, you can see virtue in how their children treat others. Money doesn't make one rich, but it is good to want it all when it comes to doing right. What sort of power could bring a humanitarian to the brink of suicide?

One Human Being

They cannot stand it when someone has something they cannot have. They become frustrated and warped in their minds and in the understanding of their souls. They are proud to hate and not ashamed to be hated. "Starry-eyed dreamers in a train going nowhere" is how they describe anyone who thinks differently than they do.

Narcissism is a personality disorder in which one has an inflated sense of one's own importance, believing oneself superior to others.

Narcissists have no regard for other people's interests or feelings. They also have neither realization nor truthfulness about themselves. They live in a world of lies. It is often fame and fortune that keeps the wheels of relationships oiled in their orbit. They are shameless, although shame lurks in them. They do not have the ability to process shame in a healthy way.

In a form of magical thinking, they see themselves as perfect and always pass blame onto others. They are arrogant. They often feel deflated, and reinflate themselves by joking about or degrading others. Envy is their constant companion. They are motivated to get what others have. They possess an entitlement that they are more special and deserve it all. They have no boundaries and will break every rule as they walk over anyone and jeopardize any relationship to get what they want.

This mental disorder only escalates. There is no hope for a cure, because in a narcissist's eyes, it is everyone else who is at fault and needs help. This mental state causes a lot of pain not only for the narcissists, but also for everyone who must be around them. Many have fallen to the traps and snares of narcissism. Innocents start to think it is their thoughts that are crazy, but in truth the insanity is the influence of the diabolical narcissist who is driving the innocents straight to the end of their rope.

The narcissist not only knows what's going on, he is taking pleasure in it. With smiles and charm, the self-centered, money grubbing, undermining narcissist knows how to get his way. It is not only his enjoyment, but also his lifestyle. When a door of opportunity opens, he is quick to take the blameless prey, not flinching at the harm involved. The outcome is sad because one can never know what the potential of a narcissist could have been in life, or the potential of his withered and broken-down prey.

> *Then said he unto the disciples, It is impossible but that offences will come: but woe unto him, through whom they come. (Luke 17:1)*

The Bridge

In a time of hopelessness, mystical, hypnotic waters can become a voice to encourage many that the water is the answer to all unsolvable problems, and the serenity of a final peace. "Jump," they whisper.

The Golden Gate Bridge in San Francisco, California, is one of the wonders of our modern world. This beautiful bridge, over a mile long, connects the northern tip of the San Francisco Peninsula to Marin County. It took four years to build and cost thirty-five million dollars. Many workers, travelers, bikers, and pedestrians now can easily cross over these waters. This great bridge, which serves so many for good, sadly has also become a magnet to hearts in despair.

Psychosis is a major depression in which one loses contact with reality. It is an abnormal condition of the mind, characterized by hopelessness, a personality change, and thought disorder.

> *Therefore now, O Lord, take, I beseech thee, my life from me; for it is better for me to die than to live. (Jonah 4:3)*

> *But he [Elijah] himself went a day's journey into the wilderness, and came and sat down under a juniper tree; and he requested for himself that he might die; and said, it is enough; now, O Lord take away my life; for I am not better than my fathers. (1 Kings 19:4)*

Sixteen hundred suicides have been committed on the Golden Gate Bridge since it was built in 1937. There are times when evil prevails, and one can become so alone and weak that one goes to a very dark place of no return. Counselors say it is a friend who listens or someone who encourages that can often tip the scale of life and death.

> *Lead us not into temptation, but deliver us from evil. (Matt. 6:13)*

Hope is a desire for some good, accompanied with at least a slight expectation of obtaining it

> *For in thee, O Lord, do I hope thou wilt hear, O Lord my God. (Ps. 38:15)*

My hope is in thee. (Ps. 39:7)

*"If you're up there and you can hear me,
show me the way, God."*

-George Bailey

*Jesus saith unto him, I am the way, the
truth, and the life: no man cometh unto
the Father, but by me. (John 14:6)*

Coming to the end of his rope, even a humanitarian needed God
to hear him and Jesus to save him. God did.

-25-

A Sequel

O Lord God of Israel, which dwellest between the cherubims, thou art the God, even thou alone, of all the kingdoms of the earth; thou hast made heaven and earth. Lord, bow down thy ear, and hear; open Lord thine eyes, and see: and hear the words of Sennacherib, which hath sent him to reproach the living God.

—2 Kings 19:15

This is a prayer by the thirteenth king of Judah, King Hezekiah. Israel and Judah had been under bad leadership for many years and had chosen to sin against their holy God. Both kingdoms were warned by their prophets, but they instead stiffened their necks like their fathers and chose to worship other gods.

Because of this great sin, God let their neighboring enemies have victory over them. On the Assyrian throne, the treacherous and wicked king Sennacherib wanted nothing more than the remnant of the Southern Kingdom—their capital, Jerusalem.

Rending his royal clothing and covering himself in sackcloth, Hezekiah humbly knelt and prayed to his almighty God.

Hezekiah succeeded his father as king. There has never been so great a contrast as between King Ahaz and his son, King Hezekiah. Both were kings of the Southern Kingdom, Judah. The similarity ended there.

God has always plainly instructed his people how to worship and live in a way pleasing to him, in a way that holds promises of protection and showers of blessings and abundant life. King Ahaz's father and grandfather were wise men and feared God. Their rule increased Judah's character and prosperity to levels unknown since the days of Solomon. But with King Ahaz, this was not so. Blatantly, God was disobeyed and his rule abandoned. Being corrupt and addicted to idolatry, this wicked king became the ultimate pragmatist who just didn't care. He was a leader who depended upon power for the moment, never being concerned about the later cost.

Because of this, there was a continual decay of virtue, and his nation only became worse. He destroyed the utensils of worship and locked the doors to the temple. He set up altars throughout Jerusalem, denying all from worshipping the one and only true God. Idol worship overspread the land of Judah, and God's way of believing was abolished. It was said that King Ahaz sacrificed his own sons by burning them alive in a ritual to the idol Malech.

The Lord was angered at this infidelity, rebellion, and terrible leadership, and opposed the administration of such an evil king. Judah during Ahaz's reign suffered greatly. It was constantly raided by neighboring countries. National sovereignty was stolen, and Judah became a vassal to Assyria. King Ahaz brought the kingdom of Judah to complete ruin by not following the good example of his father, King Jotham, and his grandfather, King Uzziah. Two generations of power, wealth, and faith were lost.

The only good this wicked king ever gave to the world was his son, Hezekiah, the successor to the throne of Judah and a shining light to revival.

Hezekiah

The successor to Ahaz was known to be another David, a man after God's own heart. Not following in his father's footsteps, Hezekiah was instead a zealous reformer. He had a genuine love for the faith and the God of Israel. His spirit was stirred against all idolatry and lack of God's rule. When one has much love for truth, one has much hate for sin and compromise.

With this new king, there was an abolition of laws that made good bad and bad good. There was an execution of all evil; Hezekiah chose to separate from his father and the malicious ways of his idol worship. His people burned incense to the brazen serpent of the rod of Moses—once an instrument of good, the creature was now worshipped instead of the Creator. Their king could plainly see the moral, physical, and spiritual virtue of his nation was gone.

During his reformation, Hezekiah feared his people might choose to rebel, as they had lived this way for so long. It was the courage and confidence in his God that became the new king's stronghold. Trust in the Lord God of Israel saw him through. Hezekiah could encourage his kingdom to purge all sin from within. Through this new king's love for and desire to please God, the people began to see the great harm sin had brought to their land.

Now it came to pass in the third year of Hoshea son of Elah king of Israel that Hezekiah the son of Ahaz king of Judah did reign. Twenty and five years old was he when he began to reign; And he reigned twenty and nine years in Jerusalem. And he did that which was right in the sight of the Lord. He removed the high places, and brake the images, and cut down the groves, (altars of other gods) and brake into pieces the brazen serpent that Moses had made: for unto those days the children of Israel did burn incense to it. He trusted in the Lord God of Israel; so that after him was none like him among all the kings of Judah, nor that any that were before him. For he clave to the Lord, and departed not from following him, but kept his commandments, which the Lord commanded Moses. And the Lord was with him; and he prospered whithersoever he went forth and he rebelled against the

> *king of Assyria, and served him not. He*
> *smote the Philistines, even unto Gaza,*
> *and the borders thereof, from the tower*
> *of the watchmen to the fenced city. (2*
> *Kings 18:1-8)*

Hezekiah's life, like all lives, was full of choices. Having such a wicked father meant his childhood home was filled with depravity. This made for a very poor father figure and example to follow.

Hezekiah's mother was Abijah, often called Abi. Her name in the Hebrew tongue meant "worshipper of Jehovah." She was the daughter of Zachariah, a well-known high priest under the rule of King Uzziah. Zachariah's name meant "my Father is Jehovah." Even though Ahaz was a terrible father figure, Hezekiah experienced stability in faith and worship from his mother and her family. Hezekiah determined at a young age that no matter the cost, he would separate from wrongdoing. With a determined heart, he wanted the same for his people.

King Ahaz was dead by the age of thirty-six, his son succeeded. In the first year of his reign, Hezekiah opened the doors of the house of the Lord and repaired them. Immediately he and his people began to physically clean house. They started with the tarnished hinges and the decayed wood. Going inside, they abolished all the dirt and cobwebs, turning the darkened rooms into light so as to view God's holy Word. The priests were then brought to the eastern street, where they heard a proclamation from their new king. "Hear me" was the message. A serious person with a serious job to do was King Hezekiah.

"Sanctify now yourselves, and sanctify the house of the Lord God of your fathers and carry forth the filthiness out of the holy place. For our fathers have trespassed and done that which was evil in the eyes of the Lord thy God, and have forsaken him, and have turned away their faces from the habitation of the Lord, and turned their backs.

Also they have shut up the doors of the porch, and put out the lamps, and have not burned incense nor offered burnt-offerings in the holy place unto the God of Israel. Wherefore the wrath of the Lord was upon Judah and Jerusalem, and he hath delivered them to trouble, to astonishment, and to hissing as ye see with your eyes. For lo, our fathers have fallen by the sword, and our sons and our daughters and our wives are in captivity for this. Now it is in mine heart to make a covenant with the Lord God of Israel that his fierce wrath may turn away from us. My sons be not now negligent; for the Lord hath chosen you to stand before him, to serve him, and that ye should minister unto him, and burn incense.

And they gathered their brethren, and sanctified themselves, and came, according to the commandment of the king, by the *words of the Lord, to cleanse the house of the Lord.*

Moreover all the vessels, which king Ahaz in his reign did cast away in his transgression, have we prepared and sanctified, and behold, they are before the altar of the Lord. In the sixteenth day of the first month they made an end and the job of cleansing and sanctification was done. It was finished. The entire congregation now could worship, singers sang, and the trumpeters sounded. The service of the house of the Lord was set in order by God's holy rule. King Hezekiah then sent letters to all Israel and Judah, to Ephraim and Manasseh; that they all should come to the house of the Lord and keep the Passover, (a remembrance of God bringing them out of Egypt into safety.) They now had freedom to freely worship him. It pleased the king and all the congregation that there was a decree sent out that all Israel was present and Judah should turn again unto the Lord God of Abraham, Isaac and Jacob. The king was strong in his convictions and ordered them not to be stiff-necked as their fathers, but instead to yield themselves unto the Lord and enter into his sanctuary which he has sanctified for ever; and to serve the Lord so that the fierceness of his wrath may turn away from them. (2 Chron. 29:3-19)

This new king surely had a to-do list for himself and his people, a list to glorify their God not only in word, but also in deed.

1. Repaired the temple (Solomon's temple)
2. Restored the articles of worship
3. Rededicated the temple
4. Reinstated the ceremony of Passover
5. Removed all idols
6. Reappointed priests and Levites
7. Commanded his people to sanctify themselves for the approval of their almighty God

> *What doth it profit, my brethren, though a man say he hath faith, and hath not works? (James 2:14)*

As always is and always will be, there was a group of people who did not take the cleansing seriously and ignored the commands of their king. Being rebellious and prideful, they still took part in the Passover feast, eating and making merry.

King Hezekiah was aware of the unbelievers and prayed with compassion for all his people. God in his infinite mercy heard the prayer of this righteous king and chose to heal and restore the whole nation. Hezekiah reigned in a way that supplied his people with their needs, and they served their God with many tithes and offerings. King Hezekiah, throughout all Judah, wrought that which was right in the sight of God. In every work and service, by all the law and commandments, this king sought God with his heart, and he did prosper. The people followed the great leadership of their king in example, and there was much comfort and gladness in the renewed kingdom of Judah.

Again One Human Being

Now in the fourteenth year of King Hezekiah did Sennacherib king of Assyria come up against all the fenced cities of Judah, and took them. (2 Kings 18:13)

A new Assyrian king came on the scene, King Sennacherib. The evil that dwelled in his soul would try the faith of the young king of Judah. Sennacherib was known for his armies, which were not only vast but highly advanced. Bloodthirsty warriors were led by a ruthless destroyer who did not hesitate to skin humans and hang their flesh on the walls as warnings to others who might rebel from his control. Armies within armies consisted of bands of highly trained swordsmen, spearmen, archers, and slingers, clothed heavily in metal-scaled vests and pointed helmets. To view these warriors charging forth would be a horror. Judah was already being forced to pay an annual tribute to this powerful enemy empire. All Judah's walled cities had been seized. Even though Judah now had a king who feared God, there is always a judgment for past sin.

King Hezekiah, in a weak or fearful moment, sent a message to Sennacherib asking what the demand would be for their retreat from his capital. "Three hundred talents of silver and thirty talents of gold" was the wicked king's answer. One talent of silver would today equal $1,940, and one talent of gold would equal $29,085, approximately. Hezekiah met the demand by gathering all the silver in the house of the Lord and all the treasures in the palace. He stripped the gold from the doors of Solomon's great temple and also from the overlain pillars. Hezekiah had restored the temple's wealth that had been depleted in his father's reign, but he knew this time the loan was for a good cause—Jerusalem.

But the king of Assyria did not keep his word.

The Assyrian chief speaker, Rabshakeh, came in the company of two generals, proclaiming a strong message of victory from their king, Sennacherib. Being a satirical genius, Rabshakeh programmed Hezekiah's men to distrust their king. He abolished their faith, assuring them they should have no confidence in Hezekiah and indeed should fear for their lives if they did not surrender their capital. In his speech, the Assyrian spokesman exhilarated Sennacherib, magnifying him as the king of all kings. This was to make Hezekiah's men believe there was no other hope than to live within the captive walls of Assyria.

> *Thus saith the king, Let not Hezekiah deceive you: For he shall not be able to deliver you out of his (Sennacherib) hand: Neither let Hezekiah make you trust in the Lord, saying the Lord will surely deliver us, and this city shall not be delivered into the hand of the king of Assyria. Hearken not to Hezekiah: for thus saith the king of Assyria. But the people held their peace, and answered him not a word: for their*

> *king's commandment was, saying answer*
> *him not. (2 Kings 18:29-30, 36)*

King Hezekiah and his loyal men, hearing the treacherous message, rent their clothing and covered themselves in sackcloth. Hezekiah then sent his men with message in hand to the prophet Isaiah:

> *This day is a day of trouble, and of rebuke,*
> *and blasphemy: for the children are come to*
> *the birth, and there is not strength to bring*
> *forth. : wherefore lift up thy prayer for the*
> *remnant that are left. (2 Kings 19:3-4)*

Seeking God, Isaiah answered his king:

> *Thus saith the Lord, Be not afraid of the*
> *words, which thou hast heard, with which*
> *the king of Assyria hast blasphemed me.*
> *Behold I will send a blast upon him and he*
> *shall hear a rumour, and shall return to*
> *his own land; and I will cause him to fall*
> *by the sword. (2 Kings 19:6)*

King Hezekiah sent orders back to the enemy. Once again he trusted wholly in their living God. It would be God who protected their capital and delivered Judah.

Sennacherib was never at a loss for a counter attack. He defied the true and living God of King Hezekiah:

Thus shall ye speak to Hezekiah king of Judah, saying, Let not thy God in whom thou trustest deceive thee, saying Jerusalem shall not be delivered into the hand of the king of Assyria. Behold thou hast heard what the kings of Assyria have done to all the lands, by destroying them utterly: and shalt thou be delivered? (2 Kings 19:10)

Now therefore let not Hezekiah deceive you, nor persuade you on this manner, neither yet believe him: for no god of any nation or kingdom was able to deliver his people out of mine hand, and out of the hand of my fathers: how much less shall your God deliver you out of my hand? And his servants spake yet more against the Lord God, and against his servant Hezekiah. He wrote also letters to rail on the Lord God of Israel, and to speak against him, saying, As the gods of the nations of other lands have not delivered their people out of mine hand, so shall not the God of Hezekiah deliver his people out of mine hand. Then they cried with a loud voice in the Jews' speech unto the people of Jerusalem that were on the wall, to affright them, and to trouble them; that they might take the city. And they spoke against the God of Jerusalem as against

> *the gods of the people of the earth, which
> were the work of the hands of men. And
> for this cause Hezekiah, the king, and the
> prophet Isaiah prayed and cried to heaven.
> (2 Chron. 32:15-20*

As King Sennacherib and all his mighty warriors planned to seize Jerusalem, the king of Judah sounded his nation and then retired to the house of the Lord. There he spread the evil king's proclamation before the Lord and prayed to the almighty, living God of Israel.

> *O Lord God of Israel, which dwellest
> between the cherubims, thou art the God,
> even thou alone, of all the kingdoms of the
> earth; thou hast made heaven and earth.*
>
> *Lord, bow down thine ear, and hear;
> open Lord, thine eyes, and see: and hear
> the words of Sennacherib, which hath sent
> him to reproach the living God.*
>
> *Of a truth, Lord the kings of Assyria
> have destroyed the nations and their lands.*
>
> *And have cast their gods into the fire:
> for they were no gods, but the work of mens
> hands, wood and stone: therefore they have
> destroyed them.*
>
> *Now therefore, O Lord our God, I beseech
> thee, save thou us out of his hand, that all
> the kingdoms of the earth may know that
> thou art the Lord God, even thou only.*
>
> (11 Kings 19:15-19)

Then came the final message from God through the prophet Isaiah

> *Thus saith the Lord God of Israel, that which thou hast prayed to me against Sennacherib king of Assyria I have heard. For out of Jerusalem shall go forth a remnant, and they that escape out of mount Zion: the zeal of the Lord of hosts shall do this.*
>
> *And it came to pass that night that the angel of the Lord went out and smote in the camp of the Assyrians an hundred fourscore and five thousand: and when they arose early in the morning, behold, there were dead corpses.*
>
> (11 Kings 19:20, 31, 35)
>
> *And the Lord sent an angel, which cut off all the mighty men of valour, and the leaders and captains in the camp of the king of Assyria. Thus the Lord saved Hezekiah and the inhabitants of Jerusalem from the hand of Sennacherib the king of Assyria and from the hand of all other, and guided them on every side. (2 Chron.32:21,22)*

When we least expect it, destruction can come. One hundred and eighty-five thousand grand soldiers were killed in the night without the assistance of any human or other natural agency.

This cannot be explained except as a supernatural event. The phrase "the Angel of the Lord" commonly applies to a theophany, God himself, in the person of the pre-incarnate Christ, manifesting himself for a very important job. He who gives life can surely take it away.

I once heard a preacher say, "Be careful how you treat God and his children. He built you up cell by cell, and he can take you down cell by cell." I have forgotten who the preacher was, but his words live on within my memory. How we treat others is how we treat God.

What a catastrophic event for the Assyrians. What a victory for Judah and their capital, Jerusalem. What a blessing for the devoted King Hezekiah. God reached from his throne to help the thrones and homes of earth. King Sennacherib departed from his dead soldiers and returned home. There, he was killed by the swords of his own sons while worshipping Nisroch, his god.

It is hard to understand the narcissistic human being, one who is never satisfied, one who always wants more, especially what is not his to have. "Why does the heathen rage?" We will never have all the answers when it comes to the pleasure of hurting another in order to gain. Narcissism started in heaven when Satan thought so much of himself that he wanted God's throne.

Now that he is cast out of heaven, his influence still dreadfully affects mankind. Having lost one throne, he now goes after another: man's heart. It may be through one bad choice, one depressed day, one false accusation, or one attack on a testimony well kept. One person can ruin another in a moment's time. Darkness does at times prevail. It is good to know the Enemy. Guard your heart; you are no match for him. He's been in the profession for centuries. Such evil loathes the character that carries with it great right and great light.

> *Charges can be false even ludicrous, while overwhelming facts and feelings of failure enlarge to the innocent. It's not where we go and what happens to us that matters all that much, what does matter is how we respond when Jesus comes to us and says, "Follow me." Suffering often is a direct result to effectiveness and suffering does hold an audience.*
>
> —Foxe's *Book of Martyrs*

> *And the Lord said unto Moses, Stretch out thine hand toward heaven, that there may be darkness over the land of Egypt, even darkness that can be felt. (Exod. 10:21)*

Two Men

One for the first time was calling out to God, wanting to believe; another was calling out to God because he did believe. Their worlds being so different, but their affliction of evil in that there could be no hope unless they came in contact with "he who is invisible," was the same.

> *If thou afflict them in any wise, and they*
> *cry at all unto thee, I will surely hear their*
> *cry. (Exod. 22:23)*

> *In my distress I called upon the Lord, and*
> *cried unto my God; he heard my voice out*
> *of his temple, and my cry came before him,*
> *even into his ears. (Ps. 18:6)*

> *The righteous cry, and the Lord heareth,*
> *and delivereth them out of all their*
> *troubles. (Ps. 34:17)*

> *By faith Moses, when he was come to years,*
> *refused to be called the son of Pharaoh's*
> *daughter: Choosing rather to suffer affliction*
> *with the people of God, than to enjoy the*
> *pleasures of sin for a season: Esteeming the*
> *reproach of Christ greater riches than the*
> *treasures in Egypt: for he had respect unto*
> *the recompence of the reward.*

> *By faith he forsook Egypt, not fearing the*
> *wrath of the king; for he endured, as seeing*
> *him who is invisible. (Heb. 11:23–27)*

Every man and woman in the Bible who saw "he who is invisible" was a person of heartache, loneliness, and reproach.

> Must I be carried to the skies, On flowery beds
> of ease,

While others fought to win the prize, And sailed
  through bloody seas?

Thy saints in all this glorious war, Shall conquer,
  though they die
They see the triumph from afar, By faiths
  discerning eye.
  —Isaac Watts, "Am I a Soldier of the Cross"

Dear Lord, I am a soldier, and the war is long. I am a warrior
fighting the enemy that doesn't end. I am a king who sees my
people will not pray. I am a prophet whom many want dead. I
am a parent and hurts prevail. Life has become great hardship.
Do you see? Can you hear me? I will keep on, and I will endure,
if every once in a while, dear Lord, you pull the curtain and let
me see he who is invisible.

Thou art the God, even thou alone.
  —2 Kings 19:15

-26-

The Path to Home

As every story has a beginning, it too must have an end, and in our last journey together, it will lead us to none other than a place called home. It was L. Frank Baum and his yellow brick road that taught children about journey. Many lessons can be learned in travel. Once again, with a childlike faith we will experience a spiritual adventure.

Stepping onto the road called Life everyone has opportunity in travel. As a child we can see examples and learn ways. It isn't far down the road that challenge comes to character, mixing personalities, qualities, and disorders. Children usually don't think beyond the present, but no matter what one's age, choices do affect one's end. Storms in our lives can sometimes make us look within and examine ourselves. What's causing our thunder?

Four beings came to such a place of examining themselves. In doing so, they discovered brokenness, void and loss. They all wanted to be fixed. It was this desire that made the impossible possible.

Friendship is a mutual attachment of affection and esteem. It involves having a favorable opinion and respect for another's worth, sharing confidence, integrity, and sincerity.

> *A friend loveth at all times. (Prov. 17:17)*

> *Faithful are the wounds of a friend. (Prov. 27:26)*

> *And there is a friend that sticketh closer than a brother. (Prov. 18:24)*

A storm wrecked her home and separated her from life and love. Meeting others, she soon learned they too had just as much need. With compassion, the child named Dorothy wanted the others to find their way too and be fixed. One path held promise. Though they were different, she and her companions became one in their travel.

A *path* can be a course of life, a narrow way beaten or trodden down. It takes one to a destination, pushes one forward. It is a course of providential dealings.

> *I have taught thee in the way of wisdom;*
> *I have led thee in right paths. (Prov. 4:11)*

> *Ask, and it shall be given you; seek and*
> *ye shall find; knock and it shall be opened*
> *unto you. (Matt. 7:7)*

The four had been given an assignment of direction and they all agreed on the willingness to trust. Even though following the right path and obeying the rules, they had been warned that wickedness was known to show up unexpectedly in all walks of life. They decided right off to believe in the promises of the path. That way, they would positively, sincerely, and regally find their way home and be fixed.

It wasn't long into Dorothy's travel before she met up with the first peculiar sort who needed help—a man made of straw, with a voice. He was in great discomfort with a stick up his back. You could see his occupation had become somewhat of a failure. Though he was supposed to be hanging in a large field to scare crows from the crop, a crow was sitting on his shoulder, picking straw from his neck.

Listening to his problems, Dorothy realized it was the fact that he didn't have a brain that bothered him the most. Encouraging the whimsical man of straw while brushing him off, Dorothy invited him to travel a road that could bring hope not only to herself, but also to a straw man in need of a brain. The Scarecrow chose to leave his old life, knowing that without a brain, he would forever be a failure. Being in need, he chose to follow a friend in deed.

To *follow* is to go after or go behind, to pursue, chase, monitor, or be a fan. It can also be to keep somebody under surveillance, to watch closely, or take the same direction; to accompany or to attend in a journey; to copy, to embrace, or to adopt and maintain the same opinions; to believe as one; or to obey as a good soldier to his general.

> *Be ye followers of me, even as I also am of*
> *Christ. (1 Cor. 11:1)*

As Dorothy and Scarecrow traveled together down the path,
they saw a Tin Woodman standing in the trees. He could not
speak nor even move. Moisture was his enemy, and left alone,
there was no one to fetch his oil can. Finding the can, Dorothy
was able to bring motion back into every joint of the rusted Tin
Woodman. Then Dorothy and the Scarecrow could hear him
whisper. He told them of his heartache. While standing in the
woods, unable to move, all he could think of was that he had
been created without a heart.

Saddened by his story Dorothy explained that the Scarecrow
had no brain and she was totally lost. As the Tin Man listened,
he was deeply moved. Seeing their compassion, he asked if he
could follow them on their path that carried a direction of hope.
"Come along," said the Scarecrow heartily. "She started as one,
and now we can be three!"

Rules are intended to make straight, control, adjust, regulate,
conform, or settle by authority. They are customs for guidance
and direction. The laws of God are rules for directing us in life,
paramount to all others.

> *Let us walk by the same rule, let us mind*
> *the same thing. (Phil. 3:16)*

The path took the companions deeper and deeper into a dark
forest. As the three held tightly to each other, a large beast
jumped onto the path and acted as though he was going to harm

or even devour them. Dorothy, thinking only of protecting her friends, slapped the beast squarely on the nose. Immediately, tears flowed down the cheeks of the great beast as he cried like a baby.

Dorothy, the Scarecrow, and the Tin Woodman were amazed at the lack of courage this beast had. The beastly Lion admitted his life had become unbearable. "I am supposed to be the king of the jungle, but when danger comes, my heart begins to beat fast. What should I do?" he asked.

The three travelers looked at the cowardly Lion and hesitated for a moment. Each one was thinking of his or her own dysfunction. They knew they too were not what they should be. After explaining to the Lion that they needed help, the group of three became four—friends who would in time become friends evermore.

> *Words are easy like the wind; Faithful friends are hard to find.*
> —William Shakespeare

Though they had been warned of evil, it was still a surprise and a shock to them all when a wicked witch appeared out of nowhere and wanted to cause havoc. They are easy to distinguish, these witches of wicked. They have bad personalities of black silk and a pointed hat, and are all green with envy. Wanting, wanting, and never satisfied, they long for more in the form of robbery. Ha-ha! It is the delight of their souls to bide their time by sowing discord and causing division. Separation is their triumph. They wear an attitude of scary and have a philosophy that is not true. They are enchanters who often speak in dulcet little voices accompanied by slivery, batting eyelashes. While they are smiling (being multitaskers), they also are making plans to hang you. When the rope is long enough, it can choke the ones you love too.

Witches have such an air; I guess *witchy* sums it up! It is hard to stay clear of the gray smoke and singed ashes of such wickedness. Simple minds and hearts can be easily seduced to fall to their trickery. Witches constantly fly in and out, following no path, and always drop in uninvited. Persecution attacks the doors of the innocent when innocents possess something these wicked ones want. It can be as simple as a joyful smile, a peace that passes understanding, or a pair of slippers.

It is a well-known fact that witches are not omnipresent and can't be everywhere at the same time. Therefore, many days are smooth sailing. It is best to appreciate these times and rest one's soul, because who would have guessed that behind every witch dwells an army of flying monkeys?

Returning home from school one day, I believed there was no hopeful solution and therefore hesitated to share my heartache. Seeing my mother's compassion, in minutes I was confiding in the one who loved me the most. A friend had abandoned me and did not want to be a friend to the very end. I'll never forget my mother's comforting words.

"Don't worry," she said. "If anyone has anything going for him or her, they best put on their seat belt, because they are going to have a rough ride."

Because I was young, my mother's counsel did not make a great impact; in fact I wasn't exactly sure what she meant. Now I understand: she was warning me of the wicked witches and the flying monkeys. I have learned it is true; they do appear sooner or later in every walk of life.

> *Teach me thy way, O Lord, and lead me*
> *in a plain path, because of mine enemies.*
> *(Ps. 27:11)*

> *When my spirit was overwhelmed within*
> *me, then thou knewest my path. In the way*
> *wherein I walked have they privily laid a*
> *snare for me. (Ps. 142:3)*

A loud screech of wickedness can harm a journey or dim the light to follow. Threatening and demeaning accusations can break one down to a state of hopelessness. Coming face-to-face with the wicked, if one is not warned, can perplex one's mind and wound one's heart so severely that a soul loses courage and will give up on finding its way Home or being fixed.

These four peculiar ones had made themselves teachable. They had become serious people. They didn't think it strange that they had to trust and depend upon each other. Their relationship with each other was the fact that they beared one another's burden and they cared. One would encourage another who had fallen. When one confessed dysfunction, another shared the burden. It was their growing compassion that made a difference. Because of their honesty, they had learned to look beyond themselves. They wanted the best for each other. Lessons on life's path they had learned, lessons that so many miss.

> *Bear ye one another's burdens, and so*
> *fulfill the law of Christ. (Gal. 6:2)*

Often feeling unsure of themselves, and many times becoming fearful, the companions didn't give up. They continued on. The rules of the way were not a burden, but instead had become a lifestyle to follow. They all shared the same vision: wanting to be right and not wanting to perish.

To *obey* is to comply with the commands or orders of instruction from a superior; to submit to direction or control.

> *Seeing ye have purified your souls in*
> *obeying the truth. (1 Pet. 1:22)*

In school we learn and then we are tested. In life we are tested and then we learn. The devilish, malevolent, diabolical witches will continue to appear on the path of life. Those who are empty hearted, missing minds, or have no courage will no doubt fall prey to these impious, wicked ones. The journey becomes difficult, and the traveler who becomes weary in well doing may be derailed from right. Testing and learning become hard or even seem impossible. When the light becomes shadowed, it may seem easier to turn back, give up, or call it quits. In these times, we need a cheerleader of *encouragement* to shout, "Keep on keepin' on!" and "You're not alone!"

> *I can do all things through Christ which strengtheneth me. (Phil. 4:13)*

> *With men this is impossible; but with God all things are possible. (Matt. 19:26)*

> *In all thy ways acknowledge him, and he shall direct thy path. (Prov. 3:5)*

A *brain* is the core of intellectual activity. A neural pathway, where many brain cells or neurons associate with each other, transmits association in order to learn. By the act of repetition or practicing our choices, the pathways deepen to become our thought patterns. These are who we are, who we have let ourselves become. Someone once said, "Be careful what you think; it will be who you become."

In order to change the neural pathway, one must strive for new strategies, rational concepts, and new methods. One must practice and practice for a new lifestyle. This is often not easy or even possible, depending on how deep the pathway has become within the brain.

Scarecrow made up his mind to have not only a brain, but a good brain. It was a choice he was determined to see through. He wanted more from his neural pathway than hanging on a pole and scaring a crow. What changed his thinking? The influence of a friend and the following of a good example. Being on the right road, obeying the right rules, and not being consumed by himself did indeed help this man of straw find a peaceful mind.

*Let this mind be in you, which was also in
Christ Jesus. (Phil. 2:5)*

A *heart* is a vital organ that keeps us alive. It beats approximately 100,000 times a day and 35 million times a year. Five quarts of blood are pumped through the lungs every minute. The blood becomes refreshed with oxygen and travels throughout the body, feeding every cell, organ, and tissue while aiding our natural immunity and muscle function. In its path of travel throughout the body, the blood's oxygen is depleted. The blood returns to the heart and is again refreshed through the lungs and sent on its way.

The Tin Woodman might not have known all the functions of the human heart. Many of us don't. But he was sure he wanted to possess a testimony of being pure and good. He knew consideration and kindness dwelled within, and one could love properly only because of the chambers of a pure heart. He wanted so to care and understand others. It was only this most vital organ called the heart that would give him his heart's desire.

The Tin Woodman experienced many difficulties and long-suffering. Choosing to follow others on the good path tested him in a way that proved his motives and who he truly was. Through his mannerisms, his tone, and his kindness, patience spoke aloud. The realness of his loyalty shone forth through a love that was rare and would eventually return to him sevenfold. The tears that rusted his joints were proof that love already lived within his chest of metal.

Many look at the outside while they marvel or condemn, but one much greater can see within—what lingers in the chambers of the heart.

> *Search me, O God, and know my heart: try me and know my thoughts. (Ps. 139:23)*

Courage is being able to do something even though it is extremely difficult or dangerous. Courage can also be the possession of mental and moral strength to venture or persevere while standing alone with one's own convictions. A great preacher once said, "never be afraid of being afraid."

Who you run with will mold your character and courage. When Lion jumped from the forest, he was beastly and rude. That's who he was, a beast. This Lion wanted to roar and have power to rule, but he also wanted to rule justly and know justice. He knew what he wanted, and he knew it was good, but his thoughts had become confused. He didn't know how to find the courage of justice.

The confessing of his weaknesses gave him power and strength. Only then could he step away from his familiar habitat and onto a path he had never known. The Lion saw he wasn't alone. He was encouraged by friends and many promises of the path. Joining a team of one accord meant a lot when his courage was tested. In the hardest of times, he felt like running back to the jungle. Instead, he watched the others, and while they stood, he stood also. With much valor, he then chose to be courageous and do right. He could plainly see there was a cause of great importance: fighting against wickedness and all evil allies. As the others fought, so did he.

Lion proved he could be courageous and that his thinking could be in all the right places. He never wanted to again be short of bravery. In his travel, he learned the true meaning of justice for all.

It is joy to the just to do judgment (Pro 21:15)

A *home* is where we lodge. It is a place we are supposed to feel safe and secure. It is where family lives. The surroundings are familiar and our needs can be met. It is not hard to find our home because we know where we live. We know the way and the address. Even a child early on is taught her home address and home phone number. All these things we learn to lead us home.

But in this story, Dorothy had lost her home and couldn't find the way. She was in a place far, far away. Not knowing the way home filled her soul with fear and a lack of peace.

Being lost affects the brain and the heart and puts a great strain on our courage. In a time like this, our brain, heart, and courage are commanded to stand at attention. A trail, a test is laid before us to see how these three will respond. Then choice makes its way to the front line, and choice determines who we are, what we do, and where we go. All trust is laid upon choice and the knowledge we have in wisdom, for we have been given the freedom of choice.

Choose you this day whom ye will serve; but as for me and my house, we will serve the Lord. (Joshua 24:15)

> *I believe no home is perfect but when lost it is missed. When gone we can surely look back and see we have been unappreciative in many ways. Seeing more clearly now of the many sacrifices and because of disbelief I became resentful when I should have been saying, thank you, I'm sorry, please forgive me and I love you. When no is the answer it is not wise to run away and become bitter but instead think and wait for the right yes to come along. It is a serious thing our brain and our heart and our soul of courage, and how we care for them. It is important they be examined on a daily bases and watched over moment by moment. Letting them go on their own can become a disaster I know. In the end more than anything I would love to go back and say how foolish I have been so many times, and that I am grateful, I am sorry and I love you for all you have done for me and others. I would love to also say, thank you because I have learned there's, "No Place Like Home." (The Wizard of Oz 1939)*

Our journey of life in the end becomes our legacy. Life is a vast testing ground of choices that will determine our standing throughout eternity. Earth is a place, a one-time chance to soar.

Many are busy seeking their own rainbows of pleasure, success, business, fame, and fortune. Others have become tired and hopeless. Day by day, they survive with no vision.

In reality, it is what's *beyond* the rainbow that truly matters. There is a place way up high, where troubles do melt like lemon drops. We cannot get there in a boat or a train, and yes, it is behind the moon and way beyond the rain.

> *The Apostle John saw a new heaven and a new earth: for the first heaven and the first earth were passed away; and there was no more sea. With guidance of an angel, I John saw the holy city, new Jerusalem, coming down from God out of heaven. And I heard a great voice out of heaven saying, Behold the tabernacle of God is with men, and he will dwell with them, and they shall be his people, and God himself shall be with them. God shall wipe away all tears from their eyes, and there shall be no more death, neither sorrow nor crying, neither shall there be any more pain: for the former things are passed away. He that overcometh shall inherit all things and I will be his God, and he shall be my son. But the fearful and unbelieving, shall have their part in the lake which burneth with fire and brimstone: which is the second death. The angel then came and carried John to a*

high mountain and he again could see the holy Jerusalem filled with the glory of God. Her light was shined as clear crystal as a stone of jasper. There was a great wall and twelve gates made of pearl and at each gate stood an angel. The city was garnished with precious stones and the street of the city was pure gold, as it were transparent glass. The city did not need a sun or a moon for to shine, the glory of God did lighten it. There shall in no wise enter into this city anything that defiled, nor worked abomination, or maketh a lie, but they which are written in the Lamb's book of life. The angel showing all this to John he then fell at his feet to worship him. The angel spoke, "See thou doeth it not: for I am thy fellow servant, and of thy brethren the prophets and of them that keep the sayings of this book: worship God. (Rev. 21: 1,8,10,11,12,21,23,27 & 22:8,9)

No longer being a child, I cannot forget the importance of the faith of a child and the lessons that can be learned.

"Verily I say unto you, Except ye be converted, and become as little children, ye shall not enter into the kingdom of heaven. "Whosoever therefore shall humble himself as this little child, the same is the greatest in the kingdom of heaven. (Matt. 18:3-4)

It is easy to change the mind of a child. Children are so often willing to learn as you explain, "Don't go there or do that or you'll get hurt." This is the process of being converted, the changing of a mind—something that is very difficult for an adult. Children, knowing you love them, will trust and believe and follow. Their hearts will lead them to hold out their little hands, knowing they are cared for. They truly believe, and their actions prove it. Humility is a lesson that is hard for an adult to swallow, but it comes naturally for small children. They, being free from pride and arrogance, want others to be built up with them, not put down so they can run alone. Oh, the faith of a child is like the kingdom of heaven.

Those who seek God will find him. If he is their hearts' desire, he will be their hearts' delight. God's promises shine upon the travelers of the straight and narrow path when they journey with the faith of a child. Believing, trusting, following in obedience, and learning to sacrifice are the markers on the map home. It is the constant examination of the brain, heart, and soul of courage that make the journey a success.

The Commander of rules shines a light of truth. Everyone is sorry and learns the importance of repentance. There truly is a home over the rainbow, way up high. You cannot get there by boat or train because it is beyond the moon and behind the rain.

> *Soon he's coming back to welcome me*
> *Far beyond the starry sky;*
> *I shall wing my flight to worlds unknown;*
> *I shall reign with Him on high.*
> —Luther B. Bridger,
> "There's Within My Heart A Melody"

The four companions knew they were broken, unfixed, and lost. They wanted nothing more than to know the way of being right. The outcome far outweighed the cost.

It is said that fear defeats more people than anything in the world. These four were guilty of fear; at times they were guilty of great fear. Instead of focusing on their fear, they chose to become cheerleaders for each other. This is what knit them together. Because they chose the same way and stepped onto the same path, their travel revealed to them and taught they had been created for a divine purpose. None wanted to miss it. Through sunshine and rain, their journey became a testimony and in the end was their legacy.

To *examine* oneself is to look with a view to discovering truth or inspecting carefully. It is to test the condition, to be right and true according to God's purpose.

> *Examine yourselves, whether ye be in the faith; prove your own selves. (2 Cor. 13:5)*

Truth is conformity to fact or reality. It is sincerity in action, character, and utterance; the body of real things, events, or facts;, fundamental spiritual reality; a correct opinion, according to God's Word.

> *And ye shall know the truth, and the truth shall make you free. (John 8:32)*

Friendship is a noble and virtuous attachment, springing from a pure source. It is a respect for worth or amiable qualities, as a well-wisher, patron, or supporter.

> *There is nothing I would not do for those who are really my friends, I have no notion of loving people by halves, it is not my nature.*
>
> —Jane Austen

> *And if one shews himself friendly, there is a friend that will stick closer than a brother. He will be your friend to the very end. (Prov. 18:24)*

Friends are not perfect. If we focus on their faults, it is easy to pick them apart. A critical spirit destroys relationships and separates those who could have been friends to the end.

I think of the friend here who was made of weathered straw, covered with bird droppings, and always falling apart. Another let himself go, to the point he couldn't function at all. When he did move around, he was noisy, clanking so loud that he could give anyone a migraine headache. Then there was the creature with all that hair full of fleas and matted tangles. Then add his OCD when it came to fear. These three needed to be fixed for sure—and they decided to follow a girl who couldn't even find her way home.

It would have been easy for them all to get discouraged and part ways. But no matter how hard the hardships became, these four had grit, guts, and determination to help one another. They let love find the way. With a bulldog determination, all four went arm in arm and chose to be friends to the very *end.*

I will be with you alway, even until the end of the world. (Matt. 28:20)

What a friend we have in Jesus, All our sins and griefs to bear
What a privilege to carry, Everything to God in prayer

O what peace we often forfeit, O what needless pain we bear
All because we do not carry, everything to God in prayer
—Joseph Scriven,
"What a Friend We Have in Jesus"

And the scripture was fulfilled which saith, Abraham believed God, and it was imputed unto him for righteousness: and he was called the Friend of God. (James 2:23)

There is only one thing greater than following the straight and narrow path, having a magnificent adventure, and reaching the glorious destination. What could it be? It would be taking others with you.

And he saith unto them, Follow thou me,
and I will make you fishers of men. (Mt. 4:19)

Epilogue

This book was not written in the luxury of solitude, but in the midst of living: a voice talking, a heart hurting, justice ignored, or wisdom proclaimed. The characters in this book carry a story of their own. Through simplicity and depth, truth and faith, they have taught me to look, seeing the extraordinary in the ordinary.

> *Let us be silent that we may hear the whisper of God.*
> —Ralph Waldo Emerson

Mrs. Roosevelt's words still ring true today. We will grow through our experiences if we meet life honestly and courageously. Life is to live, taste and experience the utmost, (a newer richer experience) for his highest.

The words of an elderly lady can change another's course in life, guiding that person to look more carefully. Time is an essance of opportunity and a good teacher finds a way that all can understand and learn, even if it starts as a whisper. To fear and not to fear is the first lesson, and then the knowing that our path is a performance, and in the end we will hear the applause of judgment and reward.

What seems even less then ordinary, in a years time looking back can become extra ordinary, how? One step at a time.

Prognosis and storms come with no invitation, but they too have a lesson that fair weather has no idea of. Great winds in the mind, though seeming not as furious, can do just as much damage. Perseverance to do right, steadfastness in hope, and determination to continue are our protection against these winds, even when we would rather give up.

It's not just the weak but the kings and the humanitarians who care that are a target for evil. Poison comes in the name of narcissism. Even cheerleaders can become weary and lay their pom-poms to the side. The world will let us down, but if we strive to be of brave heart, in the hardest times we will see he who is invisible.

Wasting even two minutes could endanger a race to be won. The greatest reward may lie in not getting one. It's the goings on of the heart that matters.

There is a shine that starts as a candle, but in time can become the testimony of a chandelier. The glow assuredly pains many. Darkness devotes its entire life to seeking the off switch. This shine serves and is changing the world one person at a time.

The art of being real has to do with compassion, truth, and justice. Bravery once again steps up to be seen, often walking alone. Real live talk will match its walk. One who shoots for the moon and misses will land among the stars.

Spirits are summoned to warn within a dream, a word and the thoughts in our daily walk. Though wickedness lives nearby, there is a greater power in love. It is dreadful and fearful to ignore whats right and the truth of it all. Not wanting to listen breeds the hardest of hearts. Surrender is the beginning to a wonderful life.

Bad words are echoed more than good. "Thank you" and "I'm sorry" and "I love you." Seldom do we speak, seldom do we hear.

One of the rarest and greatest of treasures is self-examination. It is so easy to know the faults of others. But we are strangers to ourselves. Others should be forgiven, only then do we have time for ourselves, only then can we truly look within.

Look

> *Look unto me, and be ye saved, all the ends of the earth: for I am God and there is none else. (Isa. 45:22)*

Looking is not a hard thing to do. When I was a child out walking, my mother would yank my arm. "You're not looking where you're going," she'd say. "If you keep gawking around, you're going to fall." I had many bruises, bumps, and bloody knees because I didn't look.

> *When I was a child, I spoke as a child, I understood as a child, I thought as a child:*

but when I became a man, I put away childish things. (1 Cor. 13:11)

It was the year of 1850, a young lad of fifteen coming in from a snow storm sat in a small church, alone, the voice from the pulpit told the congregation to look.

"Look, I am sweating drops of blood. I am hanging on a cross. Look, I am dead and buried. Look unto me. I rose again; I ascended; I am sitting at the Father's right hand. O look to me" were the words the preacher spoke from the Bible of Jesus.

The preacher then told the young lad how miserable he looked and how miserable he would forever be if he didn't look to Jesus. The boy didn't have to examine himself he knew he was a sinner. The Spirit had been whispering to him for a long time, but he liked his sin and ignored the still small voice of truth, until this evening.

That night, the boy was sorry for all the years of not looking. He looked unto a Saviour for his salvation. From the small town of Essex, Charles Hadden Spurgeon surrendered his heart to Jesus Christ and from that day forward one step at a time he became the prince of preachers to England, teaching all to Look.

As it is written, There is none righteous, no not one:

There is none that understandeth, there is none that seeketh after God. They are all gone out of the way, they are together unprofitable; there is none that doeth good, no not one. (Rom. 3-12)

For all have sinned and come short of the glory of God. (Rom. 3:23)

Wherefore as by one man sin entered into the world, and death by sin; so death passed upon all men, for all have sinned. (Rom. 5:12)

The wages of sin is death (hell). (Rom. 6:23)

For the wrath of God is revealed from heaven against all ungodliness and unrighteousness of men. (Rom. 1:18)

Therefore by the deeds of the law there shall no flesh be justified in his sight. (Rom. 3:20)

Where is boasting then? It is excluded. By what law? Of works? Nay: but by the law of faith.(Looking to Jesus) (Rom. 3:27)

But God commanded his love toward us, in that, while we were yet sinners, Christ died for us. Much more then, being now justified by his blood, we shall be saved from wrath through him. (Rom. 5:8-9)

Or despisest thou the riches of his goodness and forbearance and longsuffering: not knowing that the goodness of God leadeth thee to repentance. (Rom. 2:4)

Even the righteousness of God which is by faith of Jesus Christ unto all and upon all them that believe. (Rom. 3:22)

Therefore we conclude that a man is justified by faith without the deeds of the law. (Rom. 3:28)

That if thou shalt confess with thy mouth the Lord Jesus, and shalt believe in thine heart that God hath raised him from the dead, thou shalt be saved. (Rom. 10:9)

And being fully persuaded that, what he (God) had promised, he was able to perform. (Rom. 4:21)

If we believe on him that raised up Jesus our Lord from the dead; who was delivered for our offences, and was raised again for our justification. Therefore being justified by faith, we have peace with God through our Lord Jesus Christ. (Rom. 4:24; 5:1)

For with the heart man believeth unto
righteousness; and with the mouth confession
is made unto salvation. (Rom. 10:10)

Life is a journey and death we will travel also. Jesus came in a journey to live and to die. In doing so he made a way for mankind to live on with him. Jesus payed it all, all we have to do is Look unto Him, believing in his word, and trusting in him for the way to heaven. Look unto Me.

In my Father's house are many mansions. If it were not so, I would have told you. I go to prepare a place for you. And if I go to prepare a place for you, I will come again, and receive you unto myself, that were I am, there ye may be also. (John 14:2-3)

Look unto Me.

Charles Haddon Spurgeon was set apart and sanctified with a message. The ordinary become extra ordinary. A candle became a chandelier. Meeting life honestly and courageously his path was a performance, and brought applause from heaven. He wanted all to meet the most magnanimous Captain of all, Jesus Christ.

"Do not sit down and try to pump up repentance from the dry well of a corrupt nature. It is contrary to the laws of your mind to suppose that you can force your soul into that gracious state. Take your heart in prayer to Him who understands it and say, "Lord cleanse it, Lord renew it, Lord work repentance in it." The more you try to produce repentant emotions in yourself, the more you will be disappointed. However, if you believingly think of Jesus dying for you, repentance will break out.

Printed in the United States
By Bookmasters